T0326509

The Creativity Hoax

The Creativity Hoax

Precarious Work and the Gig Economy

George Morgan and Pariece Nelligan

ANTHEM PRESS

Anthem Press
An imprint of Wimbledon Publishing Company
www.anthempress.com

This edition first published in UK and USA 2018
by ANTHEM PRESS
75–76 Blackfriars Road, London SE1 8HA, UK
or PO Box 9779, London SW19 7ZG, UK
and
244 Madison Ave #116, New York, NY 10016, USA

British Library Cataloguing-in-Publication Data
A catalogue record for this book is available from the British Library.

ISBN-13: 978-1-78308-717-4 (Hbk)
ISBN-10: 1-78308-717-X (Hbk)

This title is also available as an e-book.

CONTENTS

PREFACE: RUSTBELT ASPIRATIONAL

Factory Lad – George Morgan

In September 1979 I returned to live with my parents after a gap year in Europe, and needed to make some quick money before starting university the following February. Newcastle, New South Wales, was a smokestack city built around the Broken Hill Proprietary Steelworks, now long closed, but which at that time employed many thousands of men, including some of those I had finished high school with the year before. Production had slowed after the world recession five years earlier but there was still plenty of unskilled work. It was dirty and hard, but the pay was good.

I applied for labouring work and promptly received a letter inviting me to an interview for a job in the 'Number One Merchant Mill'. The problem was that I only intended to stay for five months before going off to study, and didn't want them to know this. As a skinny, nerdy 19-year-old, I bore little resemblance to anyone's idea of factory fodder. So I clearly needed a plan for the interview and decided (with a youthful arrogance I cringe to recall) that I would need to conceal my instinctive eagerness, intellect and all-round talent! It would be vital, I thought, to masquerade as an inarticulate, working-class youth, slightly perplexed by the situation in which I found myself. Otherwise, I reasoned, they would see me for who I was: a high-achieving, middle-class kid, with big plans for his future, likely to grow restless and leave.

Fronting the drab company offices a short walk from the blast furnaces on a sweltering afternoon, I was summoned before a fierce-looking man in his fifties who had probably served his time on the shop floor before graduating to a desk job. He quizzed me about my work experience – to that point restricted to minor retail and clerical jobs – and I responded with mumbles and fragments, avoiding eye contact. This seemed to furrow his brow. 'So, where are you going with your life? Where do you see yourself in ten years' time?' he barked. Expecting questions like this, I responded with a flat bat 'dunno really' and let an uneasy silence fall between us. I thought it wouldn't help my cause to show too much ambition. After a long pause I volunteered half-heartedly that I might try to start up my own business. 'Oh yeah, what kind of business?'

he growled, prompting a shrug of my hunched shoulders. He slumped back in his swivel chair, his eyes widened and his face took on an expression that suggested that I might have over-egged the pudding.

At that moment the phone on his desk rang, interrupting his contemptuous stare. Wiping the sweat from my brow, I considered Plan B. Should I open up a bit, show a little more pluck? Or just stare him down? But by the time my inquisitor put down the phone he had lost his train of thought. Glancing at his watch, and with afternoon tea beckoning, he decided the interview was at an end. 'Alright, start on Monday.' he barked at me. 'Be here at eight o'clock sharp.' And with that he dismissed me with a wave of his hand. The interview had been a formality. There were plenty of jobs and nowhere near enough people to fill them.

Some 30 years later, my own children were young adults and one of them was looking for part-time work to subsidize his art-college studies. So I scanned a job website to see what sort of thing was available. One advertisement jumped out at me: 'ARE YOU PASSIONATE ABOUT PET ACCESSORIES?' it bellowed, without a trace of irony, inviting young people to apply for a marketing position. Enthusiasm and talent were apparently not enough. The prospective appointee would be required to summon up genuine *passion* to the cause of selling budgie mirrors and dog collars. A homely child-hood interest in hamsters or tropical fish, a particular fondness for the family dog, would simply not cut the mustard. Only those who could mobilize the most intimate of emotions would be suited to a career in selling pet accessories. The world had changed a lot since 1979: lumpen labour was apparently no longer required.

Dancing on Hot Coals – Pariece Nelligan

I grew up in the sort of town you have to leave to make something of yourself, and where many of the boys I went to school with dreamed of being professional footballers but ended up working in the local abattoir. Mum had a job in the fruit cannery and Dad with the council, but ballet was my thing and my ticket out of there. I trained in the local dance school and saved money by teaching the younger kids and by working in my uncle's fish-and-chip shop. When in 1995 I was accepted into a performing arts college in Sydney, I saw it (naively in retrospect) as the first step in a life plan: successful dance career and retire at 30 to become a choreographer.

So I moved to the city and trained in college from nine to six, five days a week. To pay the rent on my flat, I worked evenings and weekends in a bar. When asked what I did, I told people 'I'm a dancer', and the standard response was, 'Oh, right, but what is your *real job*?' So at a certain point

I stopped having these conversations. I stopped being a dancer and started being everything else: barmaid, waitress, slot-machine attendant, receptionist, personal assistant, office administrator, hairdresser, marketing assistant, music-licensing officer, dance teacher, internet-support worker, sales assistant and community-care worker. Of course, I had little invested in any of these day jobs. They did not fuel any dreams. So I kept the dancing flame burning but now more discreetly.

After five years of treading water and being subsidized by parents and occasionally the dole, I did what the obedient and pliable creative worker is expected to do: I diversified, I transferred my 'creative skills', developed parallel and cognate ambition. I found a job with a ballet organization in inner Sydney that drew on my experience as a dance teacher and office worker. Here I met other aspiring performing artists and their arty friends, between whom advice was freely given and exchanged. But I also tried my hand at acting and screenwriting, and enrolled at film school one night a week.

Not long into this job I received some blunt and sobering advice. One Friday evening, lubricated by end-of-week drinks, my colleagues and friends opened up about their ambitions. When I told them of my foray into film, an actor in the group responded bluntly, 'Well, you really can't work in this admin job any longer, if that's the case. You really should get a waitressing job at Tropicana café, if it really means that much to you. It's the home of the Tropicana film festival and loads of film-makers go there. I go there. You need to work as a waitress and get to know people. Quit now, and go down on Monday and tell them you want work.' So here was the proposition: that I give up the stable job to work for low pay as a waitress in the hope of being discovered – to become a creative wallflower. 'Love,' he said, 'it's not gonna happen for you locked away in an office, at a desk. You don't know anyone. You need to do it for yourself.'

* * *

This book will consider the plight of young people with creative ambitions, particularly those who were inveigled into paying for training in fields where they will probably never make a living. When they realize this, they have a choice: go back to square one and retrain in something completely different, or cobble together some semblance of continuity by transferring their skills and aspirations in more marketable but less creative directions. This latter group are what we call *just-in-time workers*. They accept the challenge of dancing on the hot coals of new capitalism, responding enthusiastically to its random gyrations, and reinventing themselves to fit the emergent vocational niches. To survive they must become *labile labour* (Morgan and Nelligan, 2014), moved to a state of heightened arousal by the prospect of serendipitous opportunity, infinitely malleable and manically eager, but ready to abandon artistic purity and singular, rigid ambition in favour of a life of *promiscuous aspiration*. In a world where intellectual property is the new oil and where innovation and creativity are the leitmotifs of the corporate world, there is a place for those with aesthetic skills, so long as they are prepared to barter them, to give them over to the service of shareholder value. Most of those who are unable or unwilling to do this will be condemned to poverty, precariousness and unrealized ambition.

ACKNOWLEDGEMENTS

Like all worthwhile intellectual work, this book is the product of long-term collaboration. The research was funded by an Australian Research Council Discovery Grant and we are deeply indebted to the gifted and generous members of the 'Just-In-Time Self' project team: Julian Wood (who conducted many of the research interviews), Sherene Idriss and Greg Noble. We also benefited greatly from the research access given to us by a range of organizations: Street University and Information and Cultural Exchange, the Networking Action for Film-makers and Actors and Technical and Further Education, New South Wales. Several other people provided encouragement, suggestions and inspiration – in particular Ros Gill, Megan Watkins, Andy Pratt, Alex Coleman, Alana Lentin, Phil Cohen and Cristina Rocha. More broadly, we are grateful to our colleagues at the Institute for Culture and Society and the Cultural and Social Analysis teaching group at Western Sydney University for providing the sort of intellectual environment where good cultural analysis can flourish. George benefited immensely from the opportunity to work on the manuscript while on visiting fellowships at the Centre for Culture and Creative Industries at City, University of London and Geography, Birkbeck, University of London.

Pariece: 'I wish to thank Chris for his ongoing support and encouragement, Kath for all the late-night discussions about creative work and underemployment, and my children for their understanding and patience during the research and writing process.'

George: 'Deep gratitude to my partner Cristina for her unflinching optimism and encouragement over many years for this work. My part of this book is dedicated to my children – Natalie, Rosa, Evan and Sam – all of whom are leading inspiring, creative lives.'

INTRODUCTION

The changes in work and working life are well known but it is worth restating them here. Contemporary Western societies (Watson et al., 2003) have seen a decline in manufacturing-industry and blue-collar work, especially in the manual trades that were the bedrock of working-class communities. For a period in the mid-twentieth century, large Fordist employers offered relatively stable and abundant jobs such that Western societies experienced something approaching full employment. It was around such stability that the citizenship and welfare arrangements of social democracy were built. Those who suffered two world wars and the Great Depression agreed to perform repetitive manual work in return for a good wage, with a welfare safety net to cover them against misfortune.

This was only a fleeting moment (Neilson and Rossiter, 2008; Campbell, 2013), however, in the history of labour. In the West, the process of deindustrialization began in the 1960s and has continued inexorably over 50 years. Although blue-collar work continues to be important – especially the building trades – there has been a shift in the occupational profile towards employment based on services, knowledge, creativity and technology. In 2005, *The Economist* reported that less than 10 per cent of the workforce was employed in manufacturing, down from 25 per cent in 1970.[1] In New York City, only eighty thousand people work in manufacturing where once a million did. Governments face the challenge of mitigating the effects of long-term decline in employment, a trend that has hit workers particularly hard.

This tale of economic restructuring can also be told in the register of working-class post-industrial melancholy. It is captured in numerous ballads of rustbelt decline and is symbolized most poignantly by cities like Detroit, where the car factories rot to the ground and many downtown architectural reminders of mid-century prosperity lie derelict, along with the dwellings that once housed the workers. The narrative of the flight of capital is familiar: the

---

1 http://www.economist.com/node/4462685.

factories have moved to the developing world and in the West we no longer make things anymore; capitalism has succeeded in globalizing the mental-manual division of labour and so the old skills learned by apprentices on the job, and the communities of labour built around those skills, are no longer required.

This process has produced an intergenerational disjunction. Where formerly children could rely on their parents, relatives and community members for vocational direction, this is no longer the case. The former aristocrats of labour – scions of working-class towns or urban villages – who could, with their employers' consent, shepherd the next generation into the skilled trades that they had practised, can no longer perform this role. The old manual work has moved to the developing world, and much of it is performed by machines/robots requiring no rest breaks or nourishment. Such developments have generated a sense of impotence and bewilderment: there are no clear road maps for working life and no foundation for aspirations and plans. Without credentials and training in new skills, the best that young people can hope for is to find jobs waiting tables, staffing counters and reception desks, selling things in shops, driving taxis. But for those who have emerged blinking from the post-industrial fog, precisely what those new skills are, and how much you can trust them to build a life around, remains a mystery.

So capital and labour in the West share an interest in economic renewal but it is not clear what form this will take. In the late twentieth century the so-called 'knowledge economy' was to be a source of salvation. Robert Reich's book, *The Work of Nations* (1993), crystallized the arguments for long-run structural economic change, identifying the growing importance of 'symbolic analysts', or those who work with their minds on information or symbols. By the early part of this century, creativity rather than knowledge became the key buzz-word for regeneration. In his book *The Rise of the Creative Class* (2003), Richard Florida argued that the fate of cities and nations depends on the presence of creative workers. The idea was so popular that it sparked a frenzied (and often fruitless) courtship of these trophy workers as policymakers became convinced that Florida had formulated a master code for regeneration – urban, regional and national. This is true not only in the West but also in developing economies, where creativity is seen as a key to fast-track modernization, as well as in China, where creativity is seen as a necessary step in the passage from a low-labour cost-manufacturing centre to a new economy (Ross, 2009, ch. 2).

As digital technologies render much labour obsolete, politicians are looking for things to fuel popular optimism. They argue that creativity will produce a bounty of intellectual property, the benefits of which will 'trickle down' to all. But there is growing popular scepticism in these sorts of pronouncements. The project of Western modernity – market-led economic growth, free trade, globalization – is becoming frayed. The evidence of growing disparity in wealth in the West, famously documented by Thomas Piketty (2014), seems to be reflected in the political obstreperousness of the poor and disenfranchised and in the rise of grassroots protest movements, and of popular figures on the left – like Bernie Sanders and Jeremy Corbyn – and on the right – with Donald Trump, Pauline Hanson and Nigel Farage. Working people, it appears, have yet to be convinced of the ability of the Western nation state to oversee the sort of social and economic renewal that includes them.

Measuring Creativity

It has become commonplace for policymakers to spruik the potential of the creative economy. For example, the draft National Cultural Policy paper released in 2011 by the Labor government in Australia recited a familiar mantra.

> A new National Cultural Policy will set out a framework that recognises and builds on the successes of the past 40 years to ensure that Australia embeds its creative skills and talent, not just at the heart of our cultural life, but at the heart of our technological development and national economic growth. (Office for the Arts 2011, p. 4)

This elision of art and economy echoes similar statements and policy pronouncements around the world. Creativity is the only game in town, and the desire to foster creative industries is now central to education, urban planning and social policy. In many societies, governments have redirected public funding for 'community arts' and 'community cultural development', designed to foster collective enrichment, towards 'creative training'. This accords with the neo-liberal push to reskill workers in order to kick-start the new economy. But for all the policy boosterism, the dimensions of the so-called creative economy are unclear and difficult to measure. This is because there are debates about what counts as a 'creative industry' and which sort of work can be classified as creative, both within those industries and outside. Policymakers and researchers can often find themselves at cross-purposes because the criteria used to make sense of creative employment vary from place to place, context to context.

The optimists generally embrace a broad definition of creativity. Florida, for example, argues that creative workers are those who create 'new ideas, new technology and/or new creative content' (2003, p. 8), and 'engage in complex problem solving' practice (Florida, 2003, p. 8). Such breadth has been endorsed by the UK's Department of Culture, Media and Sport (DCMS), which defines 'creative industries' as 'activities which have their origin in individual creativity, skill and talent and which have the potential for wealth and job creation through generation and exploitation of intellectual property' (CITF, 2001). This definition has been widely adopted in different parts of the world. Advertising, architecture, arts and antique markets, crafts, design, fashion, film, software, music, television and radio, performing arts and publishing are all sectors identified as 'creative' in the UK and Australia (CCI) (DCMS, 1998, 2001; CIIC, 2013) Haukka claims that in 2007/08, the Australian creative industries contributed $31.1 billion in industry gross product to the Australian economy; that is, $18.1 billion more than in 1994, yet there is still not enough work to go around (Haukka, 2011, p. 41).

Others are more circumspect. Hesmondhalgh and Baker, for example, caution against lumping together knowledge workers in general and 'symbol-makers' in particular (2011, p. 9). Elsewhere, Hesmondhalgh (2007, p. 12) defines the 'core cultural industries' as follows: broadcasting – radio, television (in all its forms – cable, satellite and digital); the film industries – DVD, other formats and television; internet content; music industries – recording, publishing and live music; print and electronic publishing – books, online databases, services, magazines and newspapers; video and computer games; and advertising and marketing with a focus on the creative aspects and the production of text that represent life. He suggests that cultural industries should also be defined as using industrial rather than artisanal/craft work methods to produce commodities – artefacts and texts, in a broad sense.

Those seeking to paint a healthy picture of the creative economy, both of the overall economic impact and of job creation, generally embrace this broad definition of the field:

> In 2006, the creative industries workforce totalled 482,700 people, representing a 5.3 per cent share of the Australian workforce and a 10 per cent growth across five years. (National Cultural Policy, 2011 p. 21)

By contrast, labour market studies of creative work, as more narrowly defined, show high unemployment and underemployment. Throsby and Zednik found that in Australia, 56 per cent of 44,000 self-identified artists ('craft practitioners, community cultural development workers, writers, visual artists, dancers and choreographers, composers, songwriters and arrangers, musicians and singers, actors and directors') (2010, pp. 15–20) earned less than $10,000 a year in creative income, and only 12 per cent earned more than $50,000. A survey of 800 UK film and television workers by Hesmondhalgh and Percival (2014) found that 60 per cent earned less than £30,000. One of the central arguments of this book is that the precarious and low-paid nature of most creative work means that those from socially disadvantaged backgrounds are less able to survive in the field. In Britain, 91.2 per cent of jobs in the 'creative economy' are filled by those from advantaged social backgrounds, as compared to 66.1 per cent of overall jobs (DCMS, 2015).

Aggregate figures of those employed in creative occupations present a misleading picture. The 2011 census shows that Australia's creative employment grew from 463,500 people in 2006 (5.1 per cent of the workforce) to 531,000 people in 2011 (5.3 per cent).[2] However, as of June 2013, the Australian film industry employed as few as 15,760, and of these only 5,639 were employed on a full-time basis (ABS, 2013). As large corporations have reduced the size of their core workforce, there is a growing gap between incomes in the primary and secondary labour markets. This is exacerbated by the increasing practice of engaging interns to perform core work, both in both creative and non-creative fields (Perlin, 2011). Powerful companies churn through aspirants who are prepared to work for free in the usually vain hope of being paid one day. Warhurst (2010, pp. 222–3) suggests that in the UK, 'overall employment in creative industries has fallen' after peaking around 2002.

The problem with the classification 'creative industry' is that it conflates creative and non-creative work (Clark, 2009; Warhurst, 2010). Many of those who perform low-paid edge-work are highly trained and talented creative aspirants who see these jobs as stepping stones – embracing the 'being there' strategy for finding a career break. Their enthusiasm quickly dissipates when career opportunities fail to open up for them. So while it may make sense to economists and policymakers to classify those who design, perform or produce alongside those who staff ticket offices or reception desks, performing minor administrative tasks, this aggregation can mask a reality of frustrated ambition. Such employment is little different from other 'Mcjobs' in the service sector.

This conflation is not simply a semantic or technical problem with the classification 'creative industry'. It goes to the heart of the creativity hoax, which suggests that you are defined by your potential – you *are* what you *aim to become* – and you can claim an occupational identity even when you make your living doing something else. The oversupply of creative labour means that most of those who persevere in the face of adversity will encounter the new economy's violent centrifuge, the force that throws aspirants, particularly those from poor backgrounds, to the remote edges of the fields in which they wish to work, or casts them aside completely. To survive, to maintain some semblance of continuity in working life in the face of underemployment or

2 The 2016 census figures are not yet available.

unemployment, often means that workers have to learn how to sell their skills in volatile marketplaces, to become entrepreneurial. Our central argument is that the idea of creative economy is in part a discursive trick concerned with promoting flexibility and mobility of labour. It deflects ambition and encourages workers to see their skills as transferable and abstract rather than particular and grounded. Like Oakley (2006), we feel there are important questions of power and inequality associated with the project of creative economic renewal, despite the fact that policymakers discuss creativity in largely technocratic and economistic terms.

This book is not devoted to detailing the political economy of creative industries – others have done that far better than we are able to (Caves, 2000; Garnham, 2005). Rather, our task is to investigate the experiences of early-career 'creatives' and how the prospect and reality of vocational turbulence shapes them as workers and, more broadly, as social and political actors in late modern societies. While analysing statistics and policy pronouncements can yield insight into the structural situation these people face, interview data can illuminate the way they respond to such challenges and how their subjectivities are shaped by them. The new economy represents nothing less than a profound change to the relations of production in the West, introducing new forms of exploitative work through outsourcing, casualization and 'flexploitation'.

The term 'gig economy' has recently entered the vernacular to describe the trend away from standard employment contracts. More workers are now living like musicians – working precariously from gig to gig. The word 'job' is losing its Fordist connotation of regular-waged work and is increasingly used to describe a particular remunerated task – such as would be performed by an independent tradesperson/artisan (Friedman, 2014, p. 172). In many Western societies, the deregulation of labour markets has promoted the gig economy, as has the emergence of websites like Airtasker, Uber X and Kickstarter, which allow prospective employers to advertise jobs of work for one-off payments, often on a competitive tendering basis (Burtch, Carnahan & Greenwood, 2014; De Stefano, 2015). This helps to explain the enormous rise in the number of small businesses (for UK data, see Bounds, 2015) in the West since the 2008 global financial crisis, a period in which real wages have decreased substantially. Companies like Uber use a business model that treats those who work for them as subcontractors rather than employees and thus avoid the obligations – for example, to provide sick leave and holiday leave – that employers traditionally carry.[3] In broader terms, gig economy has come to stand for worker precariousness and we would agree with De Stefano that

---

3 Although in the UK this claim was effectively challenged in the courts. (Osborne, 2016).

it does not represent a 'separate silo' but is part of the broader process of increasing casualization and the informalization of work (2015, p. 2). While freelance/subcontracting may suit some established, skilled and networked workers, we will argue that many aspirants are not well suited, or inclined, to meet the entrepreneurial challenges of the creative industries.

Research: Location and Method

We conducted around one hundred life-history interviews for this project, along with some participant observation of creative networking events. Many interviewees were enrolled in, or had recently completed, post-school courses in creative skills (mainly music, design, film/video) and most were from socially disadvantaged backgrounds (both working class, minority and both).[4] Around one in five interviewees were from middle-class backgrounds, and provided useful contrasts to those of the main group of interviewees, in particular in considering whether the resources they could access – social, cultural and economic – placed them at an advantage in their creative career.

Our research questions concerned the creative biography in general terms and not just the narrative of creative work. Interviewees typically described youthful creative activities as providing the seeds for their later vocational ambitions. Most of our interviewees aspired to work in the creative economy as narrowly defined, having trained/worked in music or film, with a few in fashion and graphic design. But their creative fields are less important than their disposition to flexibility, whether they were able to reinvent themselves to take advantage of opportunities, including those outside those fields, either more broadly in the knowledge economy, or as 'embedded' creative workers (Cunningham, 2013) working outside the creative industries. We were not able to assess their long-term fortunes: the degree to which they achieved some measure of creative fulfilment, some outlet for their creative skills. Budgets for academic research rarely permit such longitudinal work, but interviewing a limited number of people in mid- and late career allowed us to examine how established workers have adapted to highly competitive labour markets.

---

4 This book is based on two separate but closely related research projects. The first, entitled 'The Just-In-Time Self', was conducted in the period 2009–13 with the support of an Australian Research Council Discovery grant (where George Morgan and Greg Noble were joint chief investigators). The second was a cognate study conducted in 2009–14 by Pariece Nelligan for her doctoral thesis with the support of an Australian postgraduate award. While the first project was focussed exclusively on young men with creative aspiration, the second was a mixed sample. This explains why there are more male voices in this book than female.

This research was conducted in Sydney, but our observations about the city's aspiring creative workers, the pressures and precariousness they endure, could equally apply to those in high-rent global cities elsewhere in the world. Despite its global pretensions and popularity with tourists, Sydney is relatively peripheral to larger circuits of transnational capitalism, and like many similar Western cities, faces the formidable challenge of post-industrial renewal. It is Australia's chief centre of film, television and new media, and, along with Melbourne, of the music industry. The City of Sydney Council makes much of this, claiming that 'the creative sector' contributed a '9% share of the city's economy, with 8.3% of the employees' (City of Sydney, 2016). They represent the fastest-growing part of the economy but are much more concentrated in the city centre area than in suburban or regional centres. As we will argue below, the creative clusters – places where companies are located, networks based and work allocated – are highly concentrated in expensive, gentrified parts of the inner city. There is relatively little creative investment in distant suburban or regional areas, and aspirants from these areas are often unable to afford to live near the clusters. In the UK, too, the geography of creative industries reflects that of social class. As deputy leader of the British Labour Party, Tom Watson, observed, nearly one-third of creative industries jobs are in prosperous London, as compared with only 2.3 per cent in England's north-east, where unemployment is high.[5] This undermines the widely held belief that the new economy offers more egalitarian career pathways than those in the older vocational fields.

In Sydney, the class handicaps are complicated by those of ethnicity. More than a quarter of Australians were born overseas and those from non-English speaking backgrounds – both first- and second-generation migrants – are disproportionately represented in low-paid occupations (Alcorso and Ho, 2004). Sydney's lack of social housing accentuates the city's clear class geography, such that working people and those from minority backgrounds – particularly from the Middle East, Africa, Southern and Eastern Europe, the Pacific Islands and Southeast Asia – are concentrated in western suburbs, from which most of our interviewees come. Our study deals with creative aspirants/workers from a variety of ethnic backgrounds and our results confirm the larger patterns of disadvantage that those minorities experience. Sherene Idriss has undertaken parallel and cognate research into creative aspiration among young men from working-class, Middle Eastern backgrounds, and the various obstacles they confront (Idriss, 2018).

---

5 http://www.tom-watson.com/ccs_speech

Autobiographies of Uncertainty

A young man walked confidently into the classroom where we were wait-ing, shook our hands[6] and introduced himself as Leon. He was the first of a number of students enrolled in a sound production course that we would interview that day at a suburban technical college in Sydney's working-class western suburbs. Leon had heard that a couple of researchers were looking for interviewees and that he would be paid for an hour of his time. So he volunteered, along with several others. He was gregarious and chatty, but like many interviewees appeared slightly perplexed as to why we would be inter-ested in him. He struggled to find the correct register in which to respond to our questions. At first Leon spoke in a voice/style reminiscent of the "celebrity interview" persona. Later we speculated that he viewed our conversation not just in the terms we presented it to him – as a research interview – but also as providing a networking opportunity, a chance to promote himself. He might have read our opening ice-breaking small talk about music as a sign that we might have industry connections. But talking up your own legend takes prac-tice and chutzpah, and Leon eventually relaxed into more gentle rumination. His interview stories were peppered with self-doubt and he cut between past and present, doubling back frequently. Biographical narratives are rarely told in linear sequential fashion; rather, they are 'collagist, fragmentary, timeless' (Kuhn, 2000, p. 190), often containing conflicting elements. The formal order of realist autobiography contrasts sharply with the chaotic tangles of recollec-tion, meaning making and identity performance that make up most interviews.

By contrast with Leon, some of our other interviewees were awkward in front of their microphone, apparently reluctant to speak to us of their lives and aspirations, watchful and monosyllabic, so that at times we felt like police interrogators, facing suspects who were trying to avoid incriminating them-selves. We asked Ben, another of the music production students, about his plans and ambitions. But he was taciturn and guarded, fending off our invita-tion for him to project forward ('what will you be doing in five years time'), telling us that he wanted to keep his 'options open':

> I do have long term goals to get a good job and that sort of thing but I just keep my options open. I don't want to get tied down, I want to just see where I'm at and go from there, sort of thing.

Such diffidence has made Gen Y a regular target for media criticism. Columnists chastise them for their flightiness, lack of ambition, commitment

---

6 Interview conducted by George Morgan and Julian Wood.

and perseverance. Rebecca Huntley, for example, claims that most 'are repelled by the idea of a 'job for life', the kind of employment stability as understood by their parents and grandparents'. Gen Y members, she claims, enjoy the 'sense of freedom an unsure career path can provide' (Huntley, 2006, p. 96).

In a world where rapid social and economic change has made youth transitions particularly challenging, this would appear to be blaming the victim. To understand youthful diffidence – a condition that has been captured over a long period in texts as diverse as Salinger's *Catcher in the Rye* and Eminem's street poetry – we need more nuanced accounts. One approach is supplied by developmental psychology that views the agonies of youth as being part of a stage of life, fixed and universal, that we all go through. But this ignores the particular historical contexts in which youthful struggles are played out. More useful are the numerous contemporary sociological studies (Furlong and Cartmel, 1997; Kelly and Kenway, 2001; Wyn, 2004) on working life that argue that without the collective and institutional props that have disappeared in late modernity, young people struggle to make coherent sense of their past and future. From this point of view, structural instability produces individualism, vocational diffidence and flightiness rather than the other way around (Beck, 2000; Beck and Beck-Gernsheim, 2002).

But in looking at how people make their way through the more individualized world we need to consider narrative ability. This involves understanding the cultural factors that determine whether people can reflect on their experiences and turn them into stories to tell others and themselves – the interior narratives that are central to identity formation.

This ability is by no means universal. The great American liberal-social theorist of the mid-twentieth century, Wright-Mills, described the sociological imagination as being able 'to grasp history and biography and the relations between the two within society'. But if you have no sense of selfhood as separate from the group, then individual experience is difficult to narrate, let alone explain sociologically. Anthropologist Clifford Geertz contrasted the communal or relational selfhood of traditional, indigenous and many non-Western cultures with the Western self:

> more or less integrated motivational and cognitive universe a dynamic centre of awareness, emotion, judgement and action[...] is, however, incorrigible it may seem to us, a rather peculiar idea within the context of the world's cultures. (Geertz, 1993, p. 59)

Journalist Edgar Snow interviewed Mao Tse-tung in the 1930s during the period of the Chinese Communist Revolution. Snow wrote that Mao was sceptical about 'the necessity for supplying an autobiography' (p. 152):

Mao had talked for a dozen nights, hardly ever referring to himself or his own role in some of the events described [...] he obviously considered the individual of very little importance. Like other Reds I met he tended to talk only about committees, organisations, armies, resolutions, battles, tactics, 'measures', and so on, and seldom of personal experience. [...] [E]vents seemed to have had significance for them only collectively, not because they as individuals had made history there, but because the Red Army had been there, and behind it the whole organic force of an ideology for which they were fighting. (Snow, 1972, p. 151)[7]

If autobiography is historically and culturally shaped, then we should look at the way people talk about their lives not just empirically – in terms of the events they describe – but as texts. Each represents an interviewee's attempt to depict themselves as 'a significant agent worthy of the regard of others' (Gagnier, p. 141 cited in Kuhn 2000) and in doing so they draw on a stock or repertoire of narrative forms.

These are comprised of both the big stories that appear in popular culture – including tales of creative fame and fortune – and the small stories that circulate among families, friendship groups and communities of various sorts, and communicate values associated with collective belonging. Those who follow the creativity injunction – to 'go for your dream' and 'devote your life to your passion' – are not the tabula rasa they might imagine themselves to be when they set out. But rather they bring with them inherited narrative templates and values that shape and delimit what they can do in the public world, including in work and working life. As Clare and Johnson argue, big stories represent 'powerful sources of recognition' but we must engage in a process of 'cutting or stretching ourselves to fit' in with those stories (1986, pp. 4–5).

Contemporary neo-liberalism offers a paradox: it presents us with an apparent abundance of choice and implores us to take charge of our fate. We cannot and should not rely on following the life patterns of previous generations, but instead should construct what Furlong and Cartmel call 'choice biographies' (1997). Yet at the same time we face a future riddled with risk and precarity. In the churning, risky and unsettled lives we lead the challenge of cutting and stretching the elements of experience to tell a plausible

---

7 Anthropologist Claude Levi-Strauss once said something similar when reflecting on his own life:

> I never had, and still do not have, the perception of feeling my personal identity. I appear to myself as the place where something is going on, but there is no 'I', no 'me.' Each of us is a kind of crossroads where things happen. (CBC Massey Lecture 1977)

biographical story is formidable. Anthias (2004, p. 44) has argued that it is through narrative that people 'make sense and articulate their placement in the social order of things', but where social order is so fluid and insecure, then stories are harder to tell. As Richard Sennett has observed, this is particularly true of working life:

> The labours of the modern, flexible workplace pose quite a different challenge to the task of narrating one's work: how can one create a sense of personal continuity in a labour market in which work-histories are erratic and discontinuous rather than routine and determinate? (Sennett, 2001, p. 183)

In this book we will consider the vectors of agency and structure, examining the relative power of inherited circumstances and aspiration as the field of possibilities shrinks in front of creative workers. In particular, we will consider how inherited cultural patterns – particularly those associated with social class and gender – can encumber them. As Clare and Johnson observe, contemporary accounts of 'the self' emphasize 'flux and the fragmentation rather than the composure, the business of holding it together'. They argue that there are 'real continuities in the social relations we live in, and the cultural forms which are the raw materials for identity making. […] We may change stylistically, but unless our relationships change, the shift in style can be as easily reversed' (Clare and Johnson, 1986, pp. 4–5).

Chapter Outline

This book charts the passage from play to enterprise: from youth subculture, to creative training, to the struggles to make a living – from the sacred and expressive realms of culture to their profane commercialization.

Chapter 1 discusses the etymology of the term 'creativity' and provides an overview of the creative economy and the creative industries. We discuss how capitalism seeks to co-opt creativity and suggest the idea of creative work signifies an implicit contract between capital and labour in the interests of economic renewal. If workers consent to investing their symbolic and creative energies to commercial ends, then capitalism will emancipate them from lives of Fordist drudgery and alienation. A condition of this contract is that workers must embrace the precarious hand-to-mouth existence of artists, the occupational insecurity and uncertainty. We argue that capitalism has yet to deliver on its side of the bargain: the creative economy is more a chimera than a panacea for post-industrial ills. It has yet to deliver jobs to do justice to the creative workers' skills and inspiration.

Chapter 2 deals mainly with pedagogy and the formation of creative-aspiration pedagogical practice. The lack of employment opportunities means that more young people today remain in the education system than was the case in the past. This has led to a shift in emphasis from formal 'chalk-and-talk' academic learning towards creative curriculum and progressive pedagogy, particularly as a means to occupying reluctant learners. The chapter discusses youth unemployment and the effects of credentialism on young people's working lives. Despite the institutional and discursive processes encouraging youth towards the idea of the creative career, most aspirants eventually reach a sobering realization that this involves abandoning the sacred and ethical roots of their creativity. We consider the narratives of young people who developed an interest in either music or film during their school years, and how these interests furnished vocational ambitions.

Chapter 3 deals with the geography of creative careers, and how the concentration of work and networking opportunities in inner-urban hubs disadvantages those from socially disadvantaged backgrounds, most of whom are far away from such places and cannot afford to live there. The metropolitan journey is the stuff of youthful fantasies, but those who undertake it can encounter pressure to remake themselves, to change their image or to fit in with particular scenes and informal networks through which creative work is allocated. We show how the urban creative milieu involves the merging of professional and friendship groups – the blurring of public and private lives. We draw on our ethnographic research with a group of aspiring film-makers who come together once a month in a networking group in a Sydney pub.

Chapter 4 considers the idea of the 'day job', both as an economic necessity for unemployed/underemployed creative aspirants, and as a semantic device to distinguish between work that is temporary and disposable, and career work. This chapter will deal with the complicated and ambivalent relationship that creative aspirants have to their day jobs. We explore the ways in which the job enables creative aspirants to conserve a sense of creative purpose – waiting for their real lives to begin – but also how they live with the looming prospect that the day job will come to define them.

Chapter 5 explores the way that the habits and templates of class culture – and in particular, working class masculinity – can work against the questing entrepreneurial individualism that is central to the creative career. Men from blue-collar backgrounds often lack the characteristics required for creative career success: flexibility, individualism, opportunism and what we call promiscuous aspiration, a readiness to transfer skills and enthusiasms towards the opportunities the market throws up. Many of our male interviewees carry the cultural baggage of class that prevents them from being labile labour.

Chapter 6 looks at how creative workers resolve the experience of turbulence and precariousness in biographical narrative terms. It argues that while the creative worker is supposed to take an optimistic view of the fragmentation and diversity in their working lives, few of our interviewees are able to do so. We consider how aspirants compromise when confronted with adversity, and look at who can undertake the sort of dissimulations and masquerades required to move towards diverse market opportunities. We consider how creative workers rationalize the gulf between their erstwhile ambitions and the compromises they make in order to make a living.

Chapter 7 considers how capitalism brings creativity to market. We look at the idea of the social factory in more detail and how it challenges the work/play binary, how it makes immaterial labour 'productive' in terms of generating profit. We consider how creative people navigate and rationalize the process of becoming entrepreneurs – especially the radicals, nonconformists and outsiders. We use the term *feral enterprise* to capture a variety of entrepreneurial activities that bear little resemblance – and in some cases stand in opposition to – modern capitalism. In concluding the chapter, we will look at what forms of social, financial and institutional support are required for the as-yet-unrealized project of creative renewal: alternatives to the neo-liberal utopian fantasy that small enterprise will be the engine of future prosperity. In particular we will consider how universities can play a central role in this process.

Chapter 1

THE CREATIVE IMPERATIVE: REMAKING CAPITAL/REMAKING LABOUR

The adjective 'creative' and the abstract noun 'creativity' have been on a wild ride just lately. Where once they referred almost exclusively to artistic practice, in recent times they have become the buzzwords of new capitalism. There is hardly a corporate vision statement, a 'master plan for restructuring', or job advertisement that does not refer to creativity. Additionally, it has become a lifestyle zeitgeist in an era of increasingly precarious employment. The shelves of bookshops in hipster neighbourhoods are littered with self-help and career-advice books with creativity in the title (Barton, 2016; de Bono, 2015; Ingeldew, 2016; Judkins, 2016): *Liberate your creative instincts! Take control of your life!* A word that once signified independent self-expression has now become both a motto of neo-liberalism and a panacea for its consequences.

In one sense, there is nothing remarkable about this semantic slippage. Language is never fixed; all words change meaning through use. But this particular transition is historically important: it is symptomatic of capitalism's epochal quest to reorganize relations of production and reconstruct labour power. However, as we argued, the brave new world of the creative economy is as yet more planned than realized. Its proponents point to digital renewal, and in particular the success of Silicon Valley 'unicorns' like Apple, Google, Amazon. But there is little evidence of widespread social benefits from the tech boom. The core creative workforces employed by such companies are very small when compared with the numbers employed by Fordist enterprises in the mid-twentieth century. So without widespread reasonably paid creative employment it is difficult to argue that the benefits of the sort of economic restructuring craved by policymakers will flow to workers.

The quest to marry art and economy is formidable. In bridging the void that separates the old and new economies, employers and policymakers face the problem of how to conscript cultural energies and practices that, as Bruno Gulli (2005) has argued, were traditionally situated outside

the wage relation. Creativity is not easily summoned up by strict managerial direction. How does capitalism harness workers' ludic and imaginative
impulses, and their intellectual curiosity, to the project of building the new
economy? The inexorable logic of twentieth-century capitalism, with its
high-handed management techniques, was such as to banish culture and
creativity from the field of productive labour. We will return to this question in Chapter 7. In this chapter we will explore the different appropria-
tions of creativity by labour and capital. To understand the magnitude of
the task of economic renewal, it is helpful to consider the etymology of
culture and creativity.

Genealogy of Culture and Creativity

Although archaeological evidence – such as cave paintings and carvings on
animal bones – suggests that the human capacity for symbolic communication
is primordial, it was only around ten thousand years ago that the material conditions emerged for cultural practice in a modern sense. At this point, in the
region known to prehistorians as the Fertile Crescent, roughly congruent with
modern-day Iraq, human beings began to plant crops and establish sedentary
communities with complex divisions of labour. Such arrangements gave people time for symbolic practice and intellectual life separate from labour, and
associated with personal enrichment. Indeed, Williams (1988, p. 87) charts the
connection between culture and cultivation:

> Culture in all its early uses was a noun of process: the tending of some-
> thing, basically crops or animals […] From [the early sixteenth century]
> the tending of natural growth was extended to a process of human
> development.

He observed that in 1605 philosopher Francis Bacon wrote of the '*culture and
manurance of minds*', suggesting a metaphorical connection between the enrichment of the soil and the cultural improvement of the self. The word 'creativity' comes from a different root – from the Latin *creare* (to generate, or
give birth to). Prior to the Renaissance, as Williams (1988) states, the modern
notion of human creativity was largely unthinkable. For the most part, 'create'
appeared in the past tense to refer to God's handiwork. The word 'creatures'
was derived from the same root as creation, and, from an ecclesiastical perspective, no creature (including man) could itself be a creator. Only during the
Renaissance did the role of artist-creator become legitimate, and with it the
idea of people as originators of knowledge and culture rather than as ciphers
of the divine. The romantic idea of creativity, of the cultivation of aesthetic

sensibility, treats the work of art as a revelation of self, an expression of emotional interiority (Abercrombie et al., 1986).

Under the conditions of the Industrial Revolution, work and creativity became antithetical. As Marx observed, the inexorable logic of capitalist enterprise was to rob workers of any sense of fulfilment. Gone was the Ruskinian calm of craftwork and the satisfaction of producing the complete product because industrial labour alienated the proletariat from the products of their labour, reducing them to functionaries on a production line. At the same time, capitalism concentrates production in certain times and places. It separates work and home and orders working time around the quotidian rhythms of factory production, by contrast with the seasonal imperatives that organize agricultural labour (Thompson, 1963). Where once many of the necessities of life were produced at the household and small, local workshop level – for example, foodstuffs, textiles, clothing – gradually and inexorably these things came to be replaced by manufactured commodities.

As workers were yoked to machines, so households became primarily places where labour power was reproduced: workers nourished and rested, children raised. Feminists have observed that it was usually women who performed the tasks of sustaining and nurturing and that their life worlds were never congruent with the public/private and work/leisure divisions of space and time associated with capitalism. Despite this, the model of the nuclear family household, as primarily a place of repose and retreat, first emerged within the Victorian bourgeoisie but was gradually proselytized amongst working people in the emerging urban centres in industrial societies. The idea that cultural, ludic and leisure pursuits were separate from work has been central to modernist and utilitarian thinking, but later, as workers achieved reductions in working hours through collective action, they found themselves with more time to put to such pursuits (Clarke and Critcher, 1985).

New labour process techniques of the early and mid-twentieth century compounded worker alienation. Taylorism emerged as a creed of scientific management in the service of Fordist mass production (Braverman, 1974). It sought to achieve greatest efficiency by breaking down the production process to its smallest components, instituting a highly refined division of labour where workers perform specialized repetitive tasks. But Taylorism was also an industrial-political project, geared towards undermining the power of blue-collar trades, their skills and solidarity, and indeed the last vestiges of craft satisfaction in work. It located the scientific manager at the centre of the productive universe. In Fordist enterprises, white-collar workers grew in number and power at the expense of those on the production line and the blue-collar resentment towards those who sought so ruthlessly to divide mental and manual labour runs very deep in class memory (Watson, 2015). Ironically, at least some part of the popular reaction to Fordism's modernist hubris, to lives of scripted monotony and drudgery, has now been taken up by capital. But, as we shall see, the creative aspirations of capital do not necessarily match those of workers.

Conscripting Creativity: The Digital Bonanza

> A great lathe operator commands several times the wage of an average lathe operator, but a great writer of software code is worth 10,000 times the price of an average software writer.
>
> Bill Gates (founder Microsoft Enterprises)

If the omniscient manager was central to twentieth-century production, today new technologies have thrown a digital spanner in the mechanical works. The wealth derived from intellectual property in the digital economy vastly outstrips anything that can be obtained by selling high-quality analogue products in the marketplace. Having reduced workers to machine minders, with little autonomy and fulfilment, capitalism now needs access to vernacular culture, and must reconstruct its relations with workers accordingly. No longer can it rely on the expert in the suit as the source of all wisdom.

The decentring of management power is, of course, not completely new. The Kaizen system instituted by Toyota in Japan, and emulated elsewhere in the late twentieth century, sought to draw on workers' insights and expertise through establishing quality circles driven by the goal of 'continuous improvement' of production techniques and products. But creative capitalism effectively renounces Taylorism, and the idea that bureaucratic expertise is the unique engine of innovation, instead expecting it to emerge from below. Outside of the lush techno-burbs of Silicon Valley and a few metropolitan hubs, the creative economy remains a work-in-progress rather than something ready made and achieved.

Politicians and employers can frequently be heard lamenting the 'skills shortage', suggesting that those who graduate from education and training institutions are not equipped to match the corporate ambition. This is not simply a technical statement about matching skills to jobs, but an ideological one, a symptom of the impotence of grey-suited, leaden-footed managers trained in the dark arts of the MBA. Such people are generally ill-equipped to provide the innovation required for global competition, and they seek to shift the onus of responsibility for leading this process of renewal to those they employ (whether conventionally or through various subcontractual arrangements). In the digital age 'fast capitalism' is impatient for the next big thing, but is unclear about where it will come from.

Paradoxically, this impatience is reciprocated. For their part, workers trained in creative skills also express frustration at the lack of creative satisfaction they derive from their jobs (Haukka, 2011), claiming that their jobs do not draw on their skills and bear little resemblance to the position that they thought they had applied for. The advertising copywriter's hyperbole, once only used to sell things, is now increasingly common in staff recruitment ('Are You Passionate about Pet Accessories?'), and this serves to inflate the expectations of those who are appointed to such jobs. This suggests that the creative economy remains essentially a dream of regeneration that is yet to deliver fulfilling and challenging employment to all but a few.

A central myth underpinning this corporate impatience – explaining why the white-collar workers continue to court and humour the 'no-collar' workers– is that of the eureka moment. This describes the flash of insight – in technological, scientific or aesthetic terms – that leads to the production of vast wealth. Such stories are part of the mythology of Silicon Valley, as it has been popularized across the world. Their central characters are usually geeky, dysfunctional outsiders, people not generally suited to the rigours of the corporate career, and often not academically successful. The wayward geniuses of corporate folklore, like Mark Zuckerberg and Steve Jobs, emerge from out of the blue to challenge conservative ideas about wealth accumulation. Such narratives fuel new capitalism and help to attract venture capital. The eureka myth means that there is money available for the geeks, misfits and their hare-brained start-up schemes. It legitimates managerial faith in trailblazing but obscure research, based on the belief that there are things we can't understand about such work and that the spin-offs are potentially unforeseeable. And this means wearing the cost of the failures. For every epochal breakthrough there are a thousand ideas destined to fail.

But capitalism's needs for creative labour are not restricted to, or wholly invested in, the eureka-moment innovation. It must also enlist the support of those who can track, shape and tap the mercurial consumption patterns of late modernity. By contrast with Fordism's standardized products for mass consumption, post-Fordism generates variegated and niche-market goods and services. It is characterized not only by productive flexibility but also by complex consumption patterns, in particular because (as cultural theorists have long known!) the meaning of a commodity is transformed as it is consumed. While the standard commodity might have suited the age of mass production, contemporary consumption is now more difficult to steer and marshal. It can be characterized by irony and bricolage. Marketing is less about manipulation and more about sniffing the breeze of popular culture.

These changes are captured in the concept of the social factory – drawn from Italian post-workerist theory – which recognizes that rather than production and meaning issuing from a single point and author, this process is ongoing and diffuse. Consumers are also, in a sense, producers (e.g. as in online gaming) and that labour happens away from the factory floor in the traditional sense. The writings of cultural theorists effectively anticipated this process of improvised consumption and production of meaning (Harney, 2010; Hall, 1980). The challenge for capitalism is to discover how to profit from this dispersed creative production.

So new skills are required, new workers are pressed into service – style hunters to report on these semiotic shifts, those who design/author/perform new cultural products and those who market and sell them. Such people play a central role in the production chain because symbolic and knowledge inputs contribute much more to a commodity's value than does the labour of those on the assembly lines. As Andrew Ross (2009) has argued, art and artists – once the idiosyncratic opposites of Henry Ford's and Frederick Taylor's obedient machine watchers – are now the exemplary figures of new capitalism. They have skills and habits that were of no use on the production line but are now prized: symbolically innovative, iconoclastic and with fertile intellect. But at the same time, the definition of creativity has been stretched to include a sort of practical problem-solving savviness and, most importantly, the entrepreneurial spirit. So the new worker must not only be flexible, mobile and possessed of 'transferable skills' but prepared to lay art at the service of profit.

Capitalism's co-option of the idea of creativity is one of the more spectacular discursive operations of recent history (Reckwitz, 2017, ch.4). Indeed, the very idea of the creative economy has erased the Enlightenment legacy in which creativity is unencumbered by either commercial or ecclesiastical direction. It also conceals the bohemian tradition that associates art with resistance to capitalism. As Justin O'Connor wrote,

> Capitalism is animated by the principle of unlimited accumulation at the expense of all other values. 'Art' or 'culture' has always been one of the limits on, or protests against, this principle. (O'Connor, 2007)

As Bourdieu (1971), Becker (1982) and others have argued, artists' anti-commercialism has always been somewhat disingenuous: they have always relied on sales of their work, although this is often achieved with the assistance and intervention of dealers, agents and cultural brokers of various sorts (DiMaggio, 1977). This affords them a measure of insulation from the sullied world of commerce. In the larger sweep of history, the adoption of creativity can be seen as capitalism's response to the Left's post-1968 critique of Fordist alienation: suburban moral conformity, mass production and consumption, an alienated nine-to-five working life. Boltanski and Chiapello, in their landmark study *The New Spirit of Capitalism* (2006), argued that the key to capitalism's durability is its ability to absorb critique and deflect the social movements that challenge it, while safeguarding the core interests of the capital-owning class.

The Creativity Contract – Remaking Labour

To this point, we have explored creativity from the point of view of capital: how it functions as both a neo-liberal idiom for remaking labour power and a cure for the West's economic decline, albeit as yet unrealized. But the chapters that follow suggest that labour's conception of creativity is not symmetrical with that of capital. The history of industrialization has been one of robbing workers of any semblance of craft skill and agency, of consigning their creativity to the private sphere. So capitalism's belated conversion to the gospel of creativity is profoundly ironic. For those from backgrounds of soul-destroying and often brutal and dangerous work in factories and mines, this gospel might appear as an antidote for the hidden injuries of class (Sennett and Cobb, 1972). It is now central to the myths of popular culture – the singer who finds fame through a television talent show; the footballer whose skill sweeps the world before him (or her) – and fuels the narratives of aspiration of countless young people.

The idea of creative redemption has spawned a genre of British rustbelt tragi-comedy films (including *Brassed Off* and *The Full Monty*), of which *Billy Elliot* (also now a stage musical) is in many ways the quintessential text. It explores the relationship of working-class masculinity to art in declining industrial times. Billy's mother is dead and his father and brother are miners in a hardscrabble northern town where the local pit is under threat of closure by Margaret Thatcher's government in the early 1980s and the workforce is on strike. Poverty, flying pickets and inevitable defeat provide the tragic backdrop to Billy's story. He stumbles by chance into a dance class run by a sharp-tongued and careworn teacher whose students are all girls. After Billy shows interest and aptitude, the teacher becomes his mentor and encourages him to audition for the National Ballet School. To do this, he has to overcome the hostility and derision of the rough-knuckled, taciturn, working-class men who surround him and for whom the fine arts signify both emasculation and class treachery. But dance is a way out of the tragic trapped fate, the gruelling inevitability of unemployment and rustbelt dead-end lives. In the concluding scene, Billy's father and brother have overcome their prejudice and glow with pride at his transformation and achievement.

Such representations romanticize working-class community/solidarity, but not the work and working lives of those who lived in industrial towns who were abruptly taken from school to work in mine or mill – for example, to work the coal seams of South Wales, Yorkshire, Nottinghamshire and Northumberland. It picks up on the bitter legacy of proletarian predestination: of young men driven by poverty to follow their fathers into the pit or factory, of lifetimes of incessant toil, of occupational diseases and early death. The idea that a better life is available to those with talent, regardless of their backgrounds, is a central element of the narrative, as is the sullen resentment of those who are pitchforked into lives of hard labour and denied their youthful dreams of escape.

So, as we shall see below, working people infer from the idea of creative work an *implicit contract between capital and labour* under which the former commits to liberate the latter from mundane and repetitive work and to employ their creative skills and talents. In return for being emancipated from Fordist job-for-life monotony, workers must embrace vocational uncertainty and the state of radical bewilderment generated by fast-burn capitalism. They must accept what Boltanski and Chiapello (2006) have described as working life being comprised of a series of projects performed within loose networks rather than rigid organizational structures and communities of practice. Many of these creative jobs are outsourced to those for whom working life is sliced and diced into a series of contracts. In the dispersed and fragmented setting of the gig economy, capital relies on workers being driven not by managerial diktat but by inner drive, the realization of talent or cultural urge. Work and life are thus fused. Although retreating from Fordist-style guarantees of stability, capital's utopian vision of the new economy (the details of which we will examine more closely in Chapter 7) appears to offer the creative worker both spaces into which their talents can flow, and sufficient opportunity for them to make a living.

But while workers have taken on the challenge – training in creative skills in their multitudes –capital has yet to deliver on its side of the bargain. In the 25 years since policymakers began vaunting the prospects of creative economic renewal, the now-commonplace ambition of coupling economics and culture is still an unrealized project. Much work in the Western world remains stubbornly low skilled: based on services, retail, hospitality and the dwindling manufacturing sector. Very few workers are able to make a living from their creative skills alone.

The promise of project work has curdled into a treadmill of insecurity. Precariousness leads creative workers to adopt what Gill and Pratt (2008) term 'bulimic work patterns'. The fluctuating demand for their skills means that they are unable to decline work when it is offered to them, for fear that they might jeopardize this source of employment in the future when they need the work. As McRobbie (2002, p. 61) writes of the fashion industry,

> Working in fashion now means holding down a number of contracts at any one time, and juggling all at once for fear that one or all of them will not be renewed. Moving so rapidly across the sector and being forced to develop new expertise when fashion work drops off, the workforce loses its collective identity.

From this perspective, the collectivized aspiration of the social factory mutates to a thoroughly individualized work culture (Scharff, 2016). The solidarity that workers once enjoyed in workplaces with fixed communities of practice transmutes to a dispersed and hypercompetitive environment in which many are unable to survive. We will come back to this theme in the final chapter of the book.

Conclusion

In this chapter we have argued that creativity is the central organizing concept of economic regeneration for both capital and labour, but that, despite the apparent convergence, each is drawn to the idea by incommensurable utopias. The creativity of the start-up myth bears little resemblance to the romantic creativity, or the bohemian creativity of protest, or the Billy Elliot, proletarian self-actualization version of creativity – historic reparation for those who never had access to the meritocracy and free cultural expression of the bourgeoisie. Capital's creativity – knowledge, problem-solving acumen and symbolic work that can yield intellectual property and commodities – ignores much of the word's legacy. For labour, creativity has its roots in play and curiosity, and creative ambition is frequently grounded in the fertile period of symbolic creativity that is youth. In the next chapter we will examine the institutional and discursive processes that persuade creative youth to the idea of the creative career. The post-school years bring many to a sobering realization that the sacred and ethical roots of their creativity have to be bartered and prostituted. Many young people abandon the idea of scripted conformity of the job or career for a less foreseeable working future, but they hold a perfectly reasonable hope that it will eventually be sustainable and financially secure. In later chapters we will look at how creative aspirants respond to adversity, to the prospect and reality of poverty and unfulfilled ambition. How do they salvage a sense of vocational momentum and professional creative identity when the labour market is telling them they are no more than amateurs and hobbyists, that their talents, degrees and diplomas only qualify them to work in shops, call centres or cafes? What is required of those who, in the face of frustrated ambition, are forced to recalibrate their aspirations? What sorts of compromises must they make – day jobs, networking strategies, selling out their art? Can they conserve some sense of continuity in their narratives of vocational identity? Can they give a plausible account of their hyphenated lives?

Chapter 2

POST-INDUSTRIAL PEDAGOGY

> A democratic society seeks to unleash the creativity of all its citizens.
> [...] The value of creativity is something that is increasingly recognised
> and valued. Creativity is an essential attribute in an increasing number of
> occupations. [...] This policy aims to [...] build, produce and nurture world-
> class artists and creators [...] ensure the opportunities, training and skills
> development needed for careers in the arts and creative sectors are not limited
> by social circumstance [and] drive a culture of professional development
> that strengthens the capacity of artists and creative practitioners to be artistic
> leaders within the arts and culture sectors into the future.
> (Creative Australia, 2013)

In the early 1970s, fewer than one in three Australian children remained at
school until the end of year 12. Today, more than 80 per cent do (Australian
Institute of Family Studies, 2013). The UK and United States have also
increased their retention rates, though not so spectacularly.[1] The politicians
tell us that this is evidence of intellectual maturity, a stronger base for the
knowledge economy, that people of all backgrounds are seeing the value
of staying in formal education for longer. There is genuine family pride
communicated in the narratives of academic achievement that measure
intergenerational progress. The father, who left school at 15 to be appren-
ticed in a trade, can be proud if his son or daughter completes an engineering degree. Such stories are the stock-in-trade of the newer universities,

---

1 In 2010, 66 per cent of those who attended school in the 1970s, now aged between 55
and 64, achieved an upper-secondary education, where 85 per cent of 25- to 34-year-
olds reported achieving similar levels (OECD, 2012). Retention rates in the United States
increased, from 80 per cent in the 1970s to 83 per cent in 2010, with some reporting a
stagnation between 1970 and 2000 (Murnane, 2013), and a significant increase between
2000 and 2010 (Heckman and LaFontaine, 2010; Robinson and Lamb, 2012 ; Murnane,
2013, p. 383).

particularly those who draw their students from low socio-economic back-grounds and minority communities. They describe the project of social mobility, the realization of aspiration. But more particularly, they serve to reconcile a generation, who viewed the white-collar bureaucrat and the credentialed expert with suspicion and hostility, with the civilizing project of higher education.

But behind the good-news narratives of educational achievement is a wider sociological context: simply put, people persevere with formal educa-tion because there is no real alternative. There are just not enough jobs to soak up the number of school leavers who would prefer to work full time than to study. Youth unemployment rates have risen steadily in recent history through-out the Western world. In Italy, Spain and Greece, for example, around half of those aged 15 to 24 are unemployed (Bird, 2015). In Australia between November 2011 and January 2015, youth unemployment rose from 11 to 14 per cent in a period of relative stability and economic growth (Crofts et al., 2015, p. 8). This trend occurred at a time when the government removed restrictions on the number of funded places that universities could offer, so that there was more than a 20 per cent increase in undergraduate enrolments between 2009 and 2012.

The problem of work is not just one of unemployment, whether apparent in official statistics or latent by the growth in education, but also of underem-ployment. At the start of the millennium, just over 10 per cent of part-time workers aged 15 to 24 stated that they would rather work more hours and earn more. In Australia, by 2014, this figure has risen to nearly 16 per cent (ABS, 2014). More and more people are locked into youth-labour markets, in retail and hospitality in particular, where work is casual, insecure and insuf-ficient. As we shall see in Chapter 4, many young people who are desperate to escape the treadmill of the day job are unable to do so, because of the lack of creative opportunities. Even those who enjoy some measure of success can find themselves returning to service-sector employment when they are 'between jobs'.

The shortage of work has led to qualifications 'bracket creep'. Where once high-school qualifications were sufficient to get you a secure, reason-ably well-paid job, now even an undergraduate degree is far from enough, particularly for those who lack the family influence to open career doors for them. The term 'credentialism' refers to the introduction of manda-tory qualifications for vocations that formerly did not demand such things. So if young people do not enrol in courses (*earn or learn*, as politicians demand of them), they are likely to suffer the consequences of credential-ism. Those without qualifications will have little chance of finding lucrative, secure employment and this means that the period of de facto compulsory education has extended well beyond the end of high school. The expansion of formal education has helped to keep a cohort of young people who would once have left before the point of matriculation afloat in the system, and has helped to avoid the serious social problems associated with the mass youth unemployment.

Education institutions and educators have had to adapt to the fact that the great majority of young people who, in the mid-twentieth century, would have left at 15 or 16, now remain at school despite most having little interest in or enthusiasm for academic learning. This presents pedagogical challenges. We will argue in this chapter that both schools and post-school institutions have expanded their creative curriculum offerings precisely in order to maintain the interest of the reluctant learners. We present narratives showing that many resistant and dysfunctional children found refuge in the art or music room, or in the creative possibilities offered by digital technologies. Many are simply treading water; their teachers and families gently nudge them towards adulthood, at which point they hope that the young resisters will begin to take charge of their lives. However, in the process of occupying young people with creative pursuits at school, their ambition is kindled and many seek to base their lives on creative endeavours.

More and more young people are aspiring to work in the 'creative industries', seeking a vocational channel for their cultural and subcultural interests. Polesel and Helme et al., in their Young Visions study (2003), for example, surveyed 20,671 Australian students and found that 10.9 per cent of those students nominated 'artist' – being an artist, dancer, writer or filmmaker – as their aspiration of choice, which made it the most popular aspiration formed, closely followed by 'media', which was cited by 8.1 percent of students and included journalist, photographer, TV or radio production and graphic design. It seems that young people's aspirations are echoing political rhetoric, which continues to reiterate that 'Creative Australia' requires a 'creative workforce' where 'creative skills' are central to economic prosperity and national productivity (Creative Australia, 2013).[2] Yet the reality for many young Australians is that few find fulfilling work. We will consider some young men who developed an interest in either music or film during their school years, and how these interests furnished vocational ambitions.[3]

---

2 http://creativeaustralia.arts.gov.au/full-policy/.

3 Henri Giroux (1999) discusses how schools play an active role in the constitution of human subjects as not merely labour for capital but as cultural agents capable of resisting domination and of creating alternative worlds.

Schooldays Creativity

Nonconformist Neil

By contrast with many interviewees, Neil, in his late twenties when we spoke to him, is from a middle-class background. His siblings and parents all have degrees, although his father dropped out of high school and became a drummer with a successful pub-rock band. He later studied to be a social worker. Moved by a nonconformist rock and roll ethos, Neil emulated his father's youthful resistance:

> I discovered my dad's record collection at about you know nine years old and all I wanted to do was play guitar and drums and rock and roll, so you know but I grew up playing trumpet and saxophone.

He attended a government high school in the prosperous district of Sydney's upper North Shore, but Neil refused to apply himself to academic work. Instead, he found sanctuary in creative activities, something that, as he recalled, the school valued. This contrasts with the recollections of those interviewees from working-class schools, many of whom described the derision of their peers, and the teachers barely tolerating their nonconformity. Neil's participation in music kept going until the end of high school:

> I was very involved in the performing arts there, we would do school musicals every ... the rest of the time I just I pretty much checked out of high school by the end of year 10 even though I went there every day until the end of year 12, I more or less looked out the window and just I didn't enjoy much of it at all, I failed to see the point.

In an earlier era, this rebelliousness might have guaranteed his early exit from formal education. In his classic study *Learning to Labour*, Paul Willis showed how the resistance of young working-class 'lads' to institutional discipline guaranteed that they would leave school early and become factory fodder (Willis, 1977). Neil, by contrast, found some support amongst the teachers, despite his subcultural resistance:

> Half the teachers despised me and the other half loved me [and the arts teachers] were in that camp and would always, you know saw the good in me ... I was a punk rocker, I dyed my hair, I wore chains. ... I'd sprout various opinions on issues I didn't really have any idea about but I thought that I did.

This is a recurring theme for the rebellious kids, especially the boys. The art, design and music teachers became their mentors, helped to save them from dropping out. Neil had some kudos in the school. Unlike the hypermasculine jock culture of high schools in working-class areas, creative expression did not routinely draw the scorn of other children.

Guitar John

John grew up in a poor part of southwest Sydney. The second of four sons, his parents had steady work in low-paid government jobs, and, with little cash, struggled to raise children. They stressed the importance of financial security and stability and while John's three brothers heeded the message, John took risks his parents didn't approve of. Attending a school where sport was prized more than art, John was not interested in football and felt like a misfit. He describes becoming alienated from school. ('I had some problems in year 7, 8 and 9. I didn't know who I was but who does when they're 13, 14?') John's form teacher observed his growing alienation and invited his mother in to discuss it. John's mother looked around for something to boost his self-esteem and persuaded him to take up the guitar. While this provided some satisfaction and the basis for a teenage identity, it gave him little status among his peers. Unlike Neil, John acquired little peer kudos for his artistic efforts. He recalled the shame of being identified as a musician at school and the humiliation of public performance:

> But this whole sport thing … and it was like 'once a month we'll have this token music performance' get one of the music classes to do a performance. And you'd get the absolute shit ripped out of you once you played because … it just made you feel really crap being on stage and playing in front of a thousand other guys. Normally guys who played music were not, like, big muscly kind of football-built guys. The musos were weedy and all the footballers were big. So it was that kind of physical thing.

This confirms research suggesting hierarchies operate among young men around physique and athletic prowess (see Connell, 1995, on 'hegemonic masculinity').

The music teachers were also mired in the same stigma:

> They were just as daggy[4] as we were. I remember there was one music teacher for the whole school … he was a bad teacher. I thought he was

---

4 Australian vernacular for unfashionable/unpopular

an OK musician from what I know. Like, he knew his theory and really encouraged you if you were into it, if you wanted assistance he would help. But all the jocks just ripped the hell out of him. Like he was just the stereotypical piano-playing muso nerd, like skinny, weedy no-confidence guy working in this big macho school. He would have had other teachers rip on him for sure. Yeah.

Interestingly the teachers were subject to the same criteria of masculine cultural worth as the students. Tragically, John was not even able to bond with this man who, for all his inadequacies as a teacher, might have been a mentor. Both student and teacher were mired in the stigma associated with being musicians and isolated from each other.

John received scant institutional support for his enthusiasm. The home environment was scarcely more encouraging. None of John's brothers was musically inclined, his father was 'really uncreative' and while his mother had once learned piano, there was rarely music playing in the house: 'I suppose I found music myself and that was my thing.' John began to play with two school friends – mostly grunge music – in his spare time but at first they rarely performed publicly (other than when conscripted at school) and were reluctant to describe themselves as 'a band'. Neither of the other members was as serious about music as John, who had little interest in academic studies and performed poorly in his final school exams. John is an example of a school student who probably would have fallen between the cracks in the mid-twentieth century, abandoning the school for the labour market long before the age of 17. But the creative distraction provided by music kept him going. We will come back to John's creative career in Chapters 2, 3 and 6.

Music-made Matt

Matt's father is a bus driver and his mother died of cancer while he was in early high school. One of four siblings, he grew up in western Sydney and his father struggled to hold the family together. He resisted the confinements and structure of the academic curriculum. ('When I was doing the maths it was just … it's hard to explain, I didn't like the fact that it was so structured and we had to learn this.') After forming a band with his friends in his mid-teens, Matt gravitated towards creative subjects that involved performance. He could endure the theory but really enjoyed the practical side of his school music course:

> With the music there was only one real thing that we had to learn, which was a bit of grounding in theory. The rest of it was – you got set

assignments but you could do the assignments on whatever section of music you want to do … It gave you creative control really, it gave you control over what you wanted to do, which I think was the best part about it even when we got to choosing … because we got to choose the things that we wanted to do [in the final years at school]. I ended up being a performance major so four album songs I ended up doing. But you could also go choose to do viva voce which was a half-hour presentation and that took up two of your slots and then you only had to do two other things or you could do composition, that sort of thing.

Matt left school and entered the music production course at college. He was typical of many of the young working-class people we interviewed in his diffidence towards academic competition. Towards the end of high school, he had told his father that he was not interested in applying to go to university. He was convinced that no degree course could hold his interest for three years.

The entire time I've been learning I've wanted it to be enjoyable, I've wanted to enjoy it. If I'm going to get into a career, I'd much rather love that career and have fun doing it rather than a job where I can't really express myself, I'm doing something that isn't something I love.

Matt was drawn by the camaraderie of music – on both the performance and production sides – and viewed the enterprise as a craft rather than career (distinctive cultural formations, as we shall see):

Music is a team business … and I think that is one of the reasons why I enjoy it the most. In a band it's a team, you're all working towards one goal but you will contribute on different levels in different ways.

Later in the book we will return to Matt, and explore his efforts to retain artistic integrity in an increasingly digitized and hypercompetitive field.

The testimony of several other interviewees suggests that music generally provides a refuge for those young people whom teachers define as dysfunctional and resistant.

1) **Alex:** Interviewer Right. So, what subjects did you enjoy at school? Respondent I enjoyed music and that's about it.

2) **Ben:** I went to the local high school [in a working-class area of western Sydney]. Didn't really enjoy school but I picked up the guitar at

around 13 just as a hobby. Then I started getting lessons and I enjoyed it a lot and after a while I started thinking that I could take music seriously.

3) **Mark:** I didn't really study much … I sort of held that interest, an interest in music obviously, right through high school. So I did a couple of music classes amidst everything. As many as I could really.

4) **Jerry:** (who suffered from Asperger's Syndrome) With art I really got along with this other teacher … and I used to show her my art stuff all the time. She used to give me a lot of – she used to really praise me for it and even gave me some critical appraisals and stuff like that.

The figure of the alienated youth playing rock and roll (as symbolized by Kurt Corbain or Ian Curtis, for example) is well established in the folklore of contemporary music. While mid-twentieth-century schools might have responded implacably to young people who modelled themselves on such figures, today there are creative spaces in which their anomie can be accommodated (even legitimated). The creative distractions of school assume greater significance later when, after 'failing' to achieve sufficient grades to enter university, our subjects scratch around for something that defines them, some unconventional material with which to furnish ambition. Unsurprisingly, many gravitate to creative fields and develop creative aspirations that are stoked by the fame narratives of television talent/reality shows. Their school experiences confer legitimacy on what was, in an earlier era, defined as outlandish and extracurricular and encourage a syndrome of disproportionate ambition (Dwyer and Wyn, 2001). We now turn to film/media examples.

Tripwire Tony

Tony, in his early thirties, has trained extensively as a film editor but has struggled unsuccessfully for most of his adult life to make a living in this profession. The son of Italian migrants, a factory worker and a cleaner, he was still living at home when we interviewed him. Undiagnosed dyslexia hampered his academic performance at school but he discovered a flair for visual literacy. ('I'm good at thinking in visuals, that's how I think, mainly in images, that's why I want to edit.') This did little to endear him to his peers. ('It was an all-boys school so I guess anything arty wasn't exactly a priority for anyone really.') Like many of the slightly awkward young men, creativity was a way of coping with social isolation and vulnerability at school. The visual arts allowed Tony to work alone and he remains intoxicated by creative solitude.

At a loose end after finishing school, Tony became involved in a state-sponsored program called the 'Creative Youth Initiative' and undertook a course in film production and after two years made a short film. This spurred his ambition to work in the industry, but this remains unfulfilled. We will return to Tony in Chapter 5.

Henry Hundreds

Henry, of Iraqi background, grew up in western Sydney in modest circumstances with a father who runs a small business and a stay-at-home mother. He did poorly at school and, like many boys, was drawn to the ludic possibilities of art and digital media as a way of coping with ennui.

> It started when I was in … Year 10, I was doing art, I used to do draw. So me and my friends would just draw and we would make up crazy ideas about comic books and stuff and then in Year 11 we had this elective – it was film and video and most people picked it because it was sort of a bludge where you just sit in the class and do nothing so I thought I'd take it like another level and I start making my own short films in school and just from there sort of sparked my interest in making films … We sort of broke those boundaries we sort of made like a 'mockumentary' on the school and yeah we actually used the camera to its full potential and it's like one of the best things we've done.

An ancient-history teacher who used unorthodox methods to enliven formal academic curriculum further excited Henry's interest in film.

> It was sort of like undercover sort of teaching style, like he would bring in movies and cos I like watching movies I learned more from watching the movies. Like there was one movie I think it was called 500 hundred Spartans or something and yeah basically I passed that whole exam 'cause of that movie. It was pretty good the ancient-history teacher was great and we had a war with the other ancient-history class. We were the Celts and they were the Romans and we sort of turned history upside down.

After leaving school, Henry undertook the course in screen studies at a well-regarded technical college in Sydney. This provided him with a range of practical skills and a preparedness to be open to any opportunity in the industry that presents itself. But despite this he has struggled to find any paid professional work. We will pick his story up again in Chapter 4.

Amanda's destiny

Amanda was in her late thirties when we interviewed her and described being raised by her single mother on a meagre income, after her musician father died when she was young. They 'lived in squats, moved every six months and lived in houses with other people, all commune-like … and when we faced disaster, my mother let me paint murals on the walls'. Despite this early bohemianism, her mother yearned for some sort of material stability; she trained as a schoolteacher because 'all my mother wanted was a proper job and a house in the suburbs, but neither are terribly appealing to me'. Amanda grew up in post-industrial Newcastle, New South Wales, with strong working-class traditions. The dominant youth subcultures are surfing, skating and music. Those interested in film and other visual arts form a small, stigmatized, 'geeky' minority. For these reasons, Amanda 'stuck it out for as long as I could and then got the hell out of there'.

Amanda went to her local high school, which she says was well resourced in that it had many good teachers: 'There was a lot of opportunity to find what I needed, in terms of finding people to support your dreams.' She was an average student who chose humanities-based subjects and achieved high enough marks to pass and enrol in an arts degree at university. As much as she says that high school provided her with ample opportunity to form creative ambitions, she recalls that it was primary school that provided the context for this discussion:

> My 4th grade teacher told me when he read my writing that I could make a living out of this. [He] didn't tell me I was a good writer, [he] told me I could make a living out of it and I don't know, [that] ticked a box in my brain … and I dedicated my first book to him. … Thirty years later I rang him up and he was shocked and remembered me … that one comment from that one man on that one day to this little girl who just liked putting words together just changed my whole existence.

Amanda recalls this encouragement as providing her with a prospective vocation or career pathway. This gives her narrative a fairy-tale ending in that she says of her youth, 'I knew I had a creative destiny', but she did not want to live in poverty, so she 'was kind of at war with that'. The teacher's words, therefore, became a causal link between her upbringing, her aspirations and potential paid employment. In the end, it provided her with an alternative narrative to that of 'struggling artist', and one that allows her to discuss her bohemian upbringing in the context of a commercial career path, as we see later on. She recalls the pedagogical encouragement as being pivotal to who she is today. We will return to Amanda in Chapter 5.

Jai in the sky

The son of a Thai mother and an Iraqi father, Jai lived in New Zealand until age eight, when his family moved to Sydney and lived in a poor part of western Sydney. Like many of his peers, Jai was not much of a scholar and left school feeling bewildered and directionless: 'No one really knew what they wanted to do, the only people who did were people in the smart classes.' But he enjoyed art, and the less-structured environment of the art room was more to his liking than the formal 'chalk-and-talk classroom'. In the breaks between classes Jai and his friends played around with film. His narrative of creative free play at school was very typical of those we heard from who told us they were non-academic students:

> We were always interested in films [and] … we started watching the internet and everyone is making short films and chucking it on the net so we decided to do our own and stuff and so we went into it and got hooked and we have been doing it ever since. … We edited all our films at school and I spend all my lunch times, free periods just editing videos.

Jai's marks were not enough to get him into university. So with little chance that he would obtain a stable, well-paid job, he enrolled in a digital media course in technical college. His parents – a security-guard father and a stay-at-home mother – were not able to provide much useful vocational advice. But at the same time, they were sceptical of their son's vague creative inclinations, seeing them as ingredients for poverty and instability, the very things that they, as migrants, had sought to keep at bay.

> I wanted to get into something that involves, like, drawing … so I enrolled myself in visual media, which I wanted to do sort of like cartoon animation but my parents were like you know 'that's a bit of a childish job' or whatever. And then they didn't believe I would get paid as an animator or anything, so I went to digital media, which was probably better … you could choose between animation, TV, film-making, a lot of stuff like that.

So in early adulthood Jai developed the sort of diffuse interests and skills that should have made him well adapted to becoming a slashie, a multiskilled, versatile citizen of the creative industries. But this was not enough to get him much paid work and he has only been able to find work on the outer margins of the film industry.

Post-School Creative Training

> There are as many students recruited to performing arts and media courses [in the UK] every single year, as there are workers in the entire sector – including cinema staff, computer games salespeople and lap dancers. (Abrams, 2009)

In Western societies, not only are more young people finishing school, but more are also enrolling in post-school courses (making the normative 'transition' to adulthood typically more elongated and complicated[5]). Post-school education institutions have clamoured to meet the demand, both in the private sector – which in most societies set their own fees – and in public institutions, especially in the competitive, market-based system and especially in places (like Australia) where state funding follows students. The 'massification' of post-school education – accounted for largely by the increase in participation rates of young people from working-class backgrounds in times of scarce employment – has led education institutions to place more emphasis on the vocational utility of their credentials. In marketing their courses, institutions are less likely to stress liberal, humanist values – preparation for life – but to provide more emphasis on the leverage the qualification will provide to job-seekers. In an increasingly competitive education system, institutions engage in increasingly hyperventilated claims to attract 'customers' anxious about their future employment prospects. Numerous writers have criticized this neo-liberal drift in post-school education institutions, raising ethical questions about commodifying education when qualifications have diminishing labour market value.

Included in this education boom has been a spectacular growth in post-school creative courses designed to appeal to young people wishing to study in fields related to their subcultural interests and practices. In marketing these awards, institutions appeal to young people's imaginations and cultural sensibilities and often suggest that they will be dovetailed into creative careers (Bennett, 2009). At Western Sydney University, the web page advertising

---

5 Pierre Bourdieu observed that 'la jeunesse n'est qu'un mot' (youth is only a word), offering a sociologist's challenge to the psycho-social stages-of-life model offered by theorists like Eriksson (cited in Murgia, 2015).

music courses asks you to 'choose a future' beneath a list of industry occupations: music performer, sound designer, music therapy, composer and so forth, while a catchy acoustic song plays in the background. Additionally, there is a growing number of degrees and diplomas training people in creative industries management. ('Ignite your inner entrepreneur, ignite your innovative ideas and provide you with a higher education qualification in management of the creative industries' blurted the publicity for one such course.) Such publicity suggests that your fate depends primarily on your inner drive, your ability to mobilize a questing creative individualism. While this language is typical of education-course marketing, it is particularly apparent in the publicity for creative courses, in which the syndrome of inflated expectations are most marked.

The creative post-school education boom is not restricted to universities. Colleges both public and private are expanding their offerings with gusto. Film schools, in particular, market their courses mostly to a young cohort, with catchphrases like, 'You can reach new heights', 'Make it happen', 'You're only limited by your imagination.' The Australian Institute of Music, a private college where fees for a one-year music course are around $12,000, implore prospective students to 'Stop dreaming and start believing. Your music career starts here!'. In New South Wales, the state government compiles an annual 'skills list', which contains the various job classifications that are 'based on the skill needs of the NSW economy' (TAFE NSW, 2014). In 2014, this included 'advertising specialist', 'arts administrator or manager', 'multimedia designer', 'music professional', 'performing arts technician', 'photographer', 'public relations specialist', 'sound technician' and 'visual arts and crafts professional' (TAFE NSW, 2014). Those who choose to study at Technical and Further Education Colleges (TAFE) in fields on the list are eligible for public support towards the cost of their education. The promise of courses like these from institutions like TAFE is that they are helping

> people develop the skills they need to get a job, undertake entry level qualifications or transition to a new job. The expectant outcomes of this training are that individuals enrol in full qualifications or gain employment. (TAFE NSW, 2014)

Even with an increase in qualified workers, creative courses and the promise of on-the-job training, the problems of unemployment and underemployment remain.

Most of those we interviewed who had taken post-school training described a dawning awareness that their degree/diploma would not open many doors, either during their time as students or soon after finishing. We will consider some of their stories later in the book. However, not all of our interviewees took such courses and a few were sceptical that credentials would enhance their creative career prospects. One young man, working in the lighting and special-effects side of the live music production business, told us that there is no point in studying for his field, that technological change is so rapid as to make any tuition potentially obsolete before you are able to get a job. He suggested that the only training worth having is on-the-job training, if you are lucky enough to have a job where such training is available. Another interviewee spoke with disdain of the duration of university degrees, tying people up for three years when the film industry requires its workers to be restless and mobile, not committed to stay in one place for three years.

In addition to the limited opportunities, those graduates who did find work often found that it was not what they expected and did not draw on their skills. Melanie's film industry aspirations to were connected to her youthful subcultural interests in Japanese anime and pop culture. When a professional film-maker came to her school to speak about anime, this ignited career aspirations and she enrolled in a university degree in media and communications, training in technical skills that she assumed would hold her in good stead in the workforce. In comparison to many of her peers, she was lucky. After graduating and completing an internship in television, she was offered casual work in television, but was deeply disappointed in the routine button-pushing work she was required to perform:

> What I applied for was production and what I ended up … doing is something technical … basically record all the stuff, use the computer to set up records, set up all the media, I press buttons, you know when the presenters talk … and it's not fun at all – vision switching, I thought that there was more to it than that … you just sit at a computer and make sure that everything is on time and I think that's even more boring.

Melanie felt she had to conceal her disappointment or risk being replaced: 'They take on all the interns, it seems, for full-time jobs as technical directors.' This monotonous work proved to be a cold shower. Melanie felt she had arrived at the end of the road before she even started, that her prospects of moving into rewarding creative work anytime soon were remote. So she decided to retrain as a teacher.

> Kind of feels like I've already wasted those four years [at uni] because it's like what do I get with that, you know, what do I get out of it? Oh, I learnt how to do a few things, learnt how to use a camera better than I would've known, but I don't feel like I'm any better off. I've done a

film degree, but I don't know how to implement that; so now in the back of my head, it's just keep the creative things to hobbies and work as a teacher.

The creative training that Melanie's degree provided for her, and the fulfilling projects she was involved in with other students, had the effect of raising her expectations.

The glut of graduates in creative skills raises some thorny ethical questions for those who teach them. We interviewed AJ, who has been in charge of a music-studies course in a technical college, for which around four hundred students are enrolled:

> If I am honest I would say that we still 'over-encourage' them. And I get parents who are saying, 'I am going to be spending nine thousand on this course will my [son/daughter] have a job at the end?' … I think the ones that want to work will always work. The chances of really 'making it' are one in a million.

He contrasts the old days (when he was a jobbing musician) with contemporary credentialism:

> You got a call, you went there, you turned up and got it down or you didn't. You were judged on that and that alone. If you did all those things you got a call back, if you didn't well then you didn't get any more work. … It was a matter if you could actually do stuff and you were helpful and you didn't irritate the people that were supposed to be doing the job around you and who are your bosses really. And that is the other problem the young person with the qualification has: a tendency towards a superiority complex.

The figure of the arrogant but incompetent graduate haunted twentieth-century narratives of occupational de-skilling. Such people were the archetypal nemesis of old stagers who learned their trade on the job. But it is strange and perhaps telling that someone who teaches in an institution that confers such credentials appears to be uncertain about their value.

Conclusion: All Dressed Up and Nowhere to Go?

Many of those who, in an earlier era, would have left school well before adulthood have been persuaded to remain, in part because teachers and schools encouraged them to be creative. This encouragement has its roots in progressive pedagogy theory and artistic romanticism, but it also chimes with the wider social injunction to bring creativity into working life. However, creative work rarely matches the expectations raised in creative education – especially the free-play projects generated in school/college/university communities of practice. Once they leave formal education, graduates encounter the cold neo-liberal message that they are responsible for their fate. Creative youth should 'go for their dream' and not be satisfied with the safe option, but they must also be tactical and practical. As the sociologists of risk and reflexivity in late modernity have observed (Giddens, 1991; Furlong and Cartmel, 1997), working lives have become individualized and improvised. Workers are less able to rely on communities, institutions and skills than in the past. So the pursuit of creative vocation is a gamble, especially if it involves long periods of training. This may not be apparent to students when they enrol, but most soon become aware of oversupply, of flexploitation, of mundane jobs that masquerade as creative, of a life of long struggle.

At the stage where education gets more 'pointy', more directed at career outcomes, the institutions that offer this education have a responsibility to be candid about these vocational circumstances and not get carried away by their marketing spin. Universities have probably been less candid than colleges, relying on the idea that they have a more elevated role than simply conferring vocational credentials. But where courses are obviously geared to particular careers, and where those labour markets are oversubscribed, students often feel betrayed when they find their qualifications lack the gilt edge that they expected. This sense of betrayal is especially marked in those from working-class backgrounds, who are more likely to view post-school education in contractual terms (Connell, 2003). In the final chapter of this book we will look at how, if they observe an extended obligation towards their graduates, education institutions can begin to play a central public role in incubating creativity and priming the pump of the new economy.

Chapter 3

LEAVING COVERS-LAND: THE METROPOLITAN JOURNEY AND THE CREATIVE NETWORK

Most creative aspirants from working-class and minority backgrounds have grown up in places remote from the epicentres of the creative economy, and must undertake journeys if they are to fulfil their life plans. Such journeys are archetypal – the stuff of youthful fantasies – but they can provide both economic and social challenges. The journey forms part of the classic Bildungsroman narrative of the passage from adolescence to maturity. It is not just geographical, but also social and cultural. It can require aspirants to remake themselves, to change their image, in order to fit in with new urban scenes. The informal and improvised relations of the new economy mean that to be seen as cool or hip is not only important for accessing particular peer social groups, but also the networks through which vocational opportunities are allocated. In this chapter we argue that, far from being the egalitarian sphere that some have suggested, the new economy can actually accentuate existing power relations and sources of disadvantage. Those who are deemed not worthy rarely get far and the social and economic costs associated with ambition can be high. Our interviewees, most of whom grew up in Sydney's western suburbs, generally experience their neighbourhoods/communities as places of comfort, but also of cultural sterility, as lacking the dynamism of the creative scenes and networks that operate in the inner city. The metropolitan journey therefore appears to be crucial if they are to break into those scenes and networks and access the opportunities that might lead from them. While to the greenhorn the journey appears to offer the chance for magical change, the experience can often be demoralizing. We will look at the cases of two young women, Nada and Tanja, who, after receiving lucky creative career breaks, experience a sharp sense of cultural vertigo, of being out of place and inadequate, in their new workplace settings. With the metropolitan journey comes the pressure to make unpalatable sacrifices. They realize that, in order to get on, they will have to change the ways they presented themselves and abandon values and habits of their upbringing. The second half of the chapter will examine the creative network, its diffuseness, elusiveness and the games that aspirants must play in order to build up their stocks of social capital. For creative outliers, the challenge of building bridges into the networks through which work is allocated can be formidable.

The quixotic efforts of policymakers across the Western world to decentralize economic activity from metropolitan centres to the provinces have mostly failed. Since World War II, investment has moved centripetally, at both national and global levels. Capital cities have grown at the expense of regions – both in population and in economic terms – and global cities (Sassen, 2001) have expanded spectacularly. For a time, those in charge of renewing rustbelt cities appeared to believe they could reverse that tide. They read Florida's (2003) *The Rise of the Creative Class* and Charles Landry's (2000) *The Creative City* as implying that all that is needed to germinate the green shoots of the new economy in the post-industrial soil is to woo a bunch of artists, hipsters and start-up entrepreneurs. Unfortunately, few such people have been prepared to relocate from Brooklyn, Surry Hills or Shoreditch to Buffalo, Wollongong or Huddersfield (a town whose virtues Charles Landry extolls in his book). With the exception of the techno-burbs and hotspots like Silicon Valley, and some arcadian sea-change tree-change 'counter-gentrification' utopias (e.g. to which craftspeople who make a living selling on websites like Etsy relocate when they can no longer afford the city – Luckman, 2015), creative clusters are resolutely metropolitan.

So, as yet, neither the Left nor the Right has offered a compelling vision of economic renewal for the marginal places. Young people with talent and ambition usually work out very early on that in order to make lives for themselves, they must move towards the demographic and economic centres. Our research explored the challenges of such mobility for the outliers – the struggles they face to access, firstly, the cultural scenes and then the associated work/economic activity in the gentrifying inner-urban neighbourhoods. Although Sydney's outer western suburbs are not so far from the creative clusters of the inner city, the city's dysfunctional public transport network means that they are more remote than distance would suggest. While for most the attractions of the inner city are initially and primarily cultural – the vitality of creative scenes – those who migrate to such places very soon endure the economic pressures associated with remaining there. They must become part of the social factories of new symbolic labour, because rents and costs of living in gentrified and gentrifying inner-urban areas means that those of modest means must make a good living quickly. This presents a dilemma. Those who wish to remain in the creative clusters must *commercialize in situ*, find lucrative work or resign themselves to becoming the precarious artistic fringe dwellers, pushed further and further out of the city by the forces of gentrification.

The metropolis has long been a central symbol in the modernist narrative of youth. In the big city, young people can break free of provincialism and communal constraint, lose and remake themselves (Raban 2008). It is the centre of bohemian life, the place where you can find your tribe, where you can seek validation for being different. But increasingly the archetypal journey to the city has come to assume economic as well as existential significance. The creative cities discourse (and the idea of the new economy generally) suggests that liaisons between artists and new capitalism are central to the economic regeneration of post-industrial cities (Reckwitz, 2017). In so-called creative clusters, artists, geeks and start-up entrepreneurs mix in a highly caffeinated 24/7 public culture (Shorthose, 2004; Lloyd, 2010). From this subcultural soup arises innovations and intellectual property on which the prosperity of Western societies is said to rest. Although there is a counter-vision of neat, suburban technotopia and this still has some purchase in the wider knowledge economy, it is the case that more and more creative enterprise – start-ups challenging the business establishment (see Chapter 7) – is located in the gritty and disheveled districts on the fringes of the gentrification belt, where you can both find yourself and make your fortune – more Shoreditch, Marrickville, Kreuzberg and Bushwick than Silicon Valley, Swindon or North Ryde.

Access to this melting pot is anything but egalitarian and many discover that the streets of the city are paved not with gold but with frustration and disappointment. Most of our interviewees focussed their ambition on the creative clusters and cultural scenes that operate largely in the areas around Sydney's CBD, particularly in the inner west, that are seen as places of fertile symbolic creativity but also as sites of the operation of informal networks through which work and other opportunities are allocated. But those ambitions can be limited by the structural factors that can exclude the aspirant: high rents, low incomes and a lack of social capital that would open doors.

The Self-Assembled Creative Career

We asked our interviewees to describe the way their creative industry ambitions were formed and for the most part these were rooted in youth culture/subculture. These interests only took vocational shape as they stumbled out of the adolescent fog and were forced to face the challenge of transition to adulthood, to formulate a basis for working life beyond precarious and low-paid casual labour in retail or hospitality. Those who enrolled in post-school creative training at college level found that their courses gave shape to their ambitions and sharpened their vocational understanding. Several of the music production students we interviewed talked about the cold shower of realizing what was involved in making the transition from fan/hobbyist to producer.

Their lecturers – most of whom had industry experience – told them of the long-term freelancing life in store for them, of improvisation, entrepreneurial individualism and networking.

> It's just it's a hard industry and we constantly learn about it. Even as technical students learning about being engineers and even recording and studios or live production. That's the number one thing we learn about is that you can't just come here … and think 'I'm going to become a sound engineer.' It's about all experience and the number one thing that I've learnt about it all is your contacts, it's the people that you know. (Leon)

Ben, another of the music students, presented as being rather bewildered by the vocational challenges in front of him. He tells us that it is in the inner west that music industry commerce and contacts are to be found.

> **Ben:** Everything starts at Newtown and moves around the city – businesswise as well. There's a lot of independent stores, music stores around there so – even if you had work with then you'd get to know other people and find studios and move in through that way.
>
> **Q:** So you reckon getting a job in an independent music store would be a good career move?
>
> **Ben:** For a short-term thing, possibly. I've been looking at things like JB Hi-Fi just for casual work, that's hard to get into. That probably would be a decent place to start.

There is a good deal of pathos in this interview fragment. Aware of the improbably remote prospect of making a living in music production, Ben is casting around vaguely for an entrée, a networking strategy, that might provide him with a foothold in the industry. Awkward and introspective, he struggled to penetrate the networks through which work is allocated.

Most music industry aspirants we spoke to described participating in local music scenes, many of which happen in pop-up venues and finding audiences in online publicity through social network sites. (Ben: You always see on [social media] they'll throw it up 'so and so is having a gig tonight, come down and have a look' always just trying to promote people to get in there.) However, most also acknowledge the limited scale of the music industry in the western suburbs, recognizing that the action is elsewhere, in parts of Sydney that they have difficulty accessing by public transport. Jerry, enrolled in music production and an enthusiast of an obscure subgenre of punk tells us that he feels isolated in the western suburbs:

Jerry: There's this one guy I know that lives [in a nearby suburb and] we both share the same music interests.

Q: So … your subculture is very small?

Jerry: Yeah, very small and they all mostly live out in the city.

Leon also tells us that as a consumer, an aficionado, he has to travel toward the centre to find his tribe.

Leon: I go to these gigs, these concerts and they're there, they know that what they're there for and we can look at each other, we don't even talk and they're straight up, straight away a handshake and 'how are you going?' Straight away. Yet out here [western suburbs] it's [gestures helplessly]… and the thing that people don't get, they're 'oh it's just a shitty gig whatever' but as soon as you walk in there all these people, it sounds weird but it's almost like everyone is one and it's the weird feeling that you get. It's almost like your family for the four hours.

John (one of our technical-college cohort, whom we met in Chapter 2) works precariously in the music industry and grew up in Campbelltown to the south-west of Sydney, in a working-class family, where there was very little creative influence at home or school. As we saw in the last chapter, he was counselled by a kind teacher to take up playing the guitar to help him get over a period of teenage alienation and started to listen to and play rock/heavy metal. He formed a band but was derided by his peers at high school. John wanted to write and perform original music and to find a scene in which this creative impetus was validated.

John: I moved to the inner west because it was musician friendly. It was more about originality as compared with like, covers land. Doing something out west, 99.9 per cent of the time it would be covers related, it wouldn't be original music. It would be like, 'Come in and play the latest 'bogan'[1] hits as opposed to play your own song.'

Although he struggled to pay the inner city rents, John was able to gain a foothold in areas that most of our younger interviewees – stay-at-home Gen Ys like Leon – have little hope of moving to:

Q: Why do you keep living out here? Because you can't afford to live in the inner city?

---

1 A pejorative term, the British equivalent of which would be chav, in the United States, 'white trash'.

Leon: I keep living out here because my parents live out here.

Q: But if you could afford to live in the city?

Leon: Yeah I'd be fucking off straight to the city. I'd love it … I prefer
it. I'm not going to say that people are bad out here, they're wonderful people but … the whole thing of pretending to be a friend with
someone because they're there or actually finding someone that you
can take seriously – that's why I enjoy the city, we just constantly go to
the city because the people in the city are just so exactly what we see.

Leon inveighs against the randomness of suburban co-presence, and yearns
for the metropolitan spaces in which tribes can be formed, accidental communities differentiated.

These sentiments – those of John and Leon – echo the long-standing bohemian
critique of Australian suburbia summarized well by Hugh Stretton as the 'dreary
dormitories where life shrivels, festers, taps its foot in family prisons' (1989: p. 10).
Patrick White derided the clockwork routine, parochialism and ennui of suburban
life in his play *Season at Sarsaparilla*. Barry Humphries's Dame Edna Everage is
cheerfully oblivious to the hierarchies of taste and social distinction. Humphries
invites us to take ironic pleasure at her naïve vulgarity. The suburb, he suggests,
anaesthetizes taste and intellect; suburbanites lose the ability to discriminate
between the trivial and the weighty, an observation reprised in the television com-
edy *Kath and Kim*, depicting a mother and daughter obsessed with petty suburban
melodramas. For suburban working-class youth, creative aspiration is tied to the
project of social mobility, but not in a conventional sense. Rather, the new economy appears to allow them a new, subcultural way to be middle class, to avoid the
route taken by parvenu suburbanites. It is one thing to accumulate what Sarah
Thornton (1995) refers to as subcultural capital, but the youthful scenes in which
such capital is meaningful are rarely sufficient to build adult life.

Rites of Passage

In undertaking the metropolitan journey, and making a new life, the subur-
ban/provincial creative aspirant must depart from their comfort zone. Being a
cultural enthusiast, an expert in some symbolic field might help to open some
doors, but such talents are not enough and aspirants will often have to endure
judgements of their cultural worth. To be accepted in a professional network,
and to be accepted for employment, can involve becoming familiar with new
patterns of social distinction. Cultural judgement can come in many forms –
not necessarily through established elite or petit-bourgeois norms. Some of
our interviews, spoke of the experience of cultural pressure. We will take two
examples: those of Nada and Tanja.

The devil wears Nada

Nada exemplifies something of the heady cultural rush and excitement experienced by those who are presented with an apparently glittering opportunity in a creative field. A young woman, the daughter of an unskilled manual labourer, from a poor Palestinian-migrant-background family, she excelled academically at school but dropped out of her science degree in the first year of university, more interested in music than study. At a loose end, she went to work in a clothing shop in Sydney's gentrified eastern suburbs, but saw it only as temporary while she decided what to do with her life. The serendipitous moment came upon her when she met a woman who had set up a company in the online music business, and who recognized Nada's spark and intelligence. She was immediately seduced by the gaudy promise of a job.

> **Nada:** I met her through a customer, when I was working in Bondi … [for an] Asian clothing company … she kept saying, 'What are you doing in retail, you've got a brain.' I'm like, 'You know, I'm just trying to work out what I need to do' … I was manager in that store. I'd only been there for under a year and I was managing their flagship store. And I had better sales than everybody else. When I told them I was leaving they all tried to bribe me to stay, but I was like, 'this is going to be a great job' because this lady was going to use me as her recruit. She was going to send me to musical events and get me to recruit new people to the website. Fly me to here, and fly me to there. I did get sucked in, I think … And I put too much trust in her… She was contracting web designers, the website was already up, she had support from [a trans-national music company]…. This was my ticket to shine.

This is a story of magical happenstance – a chance meeting was the means by which Nada's potential was recognized, and produced what she saw as a turning point in her life. A young woman marking time, with talents not utilized in her shop job. A stranger sweeps her off her feet, promising a glamorous creative career. There are clear parallels here with the romance narrative (Radway, 1983), in which the figure of the innocent young woman, as ingénue or wallflower, awaits transformation by a powerful external force – invariably a mysterious handsome stranger, in the hetero-normative trope of romantic love. But the fact that the provocateur was a woman is less important than the fact that our interviewee was open to being seduced by this promise. For the most part, our women interviewees were much more keenly aware of, and open to, the possibility of chance, life-transforming encounters, than were the men.

Nada soon found that she was being judged on much more than her work performance. Her employer criticized her dress and presentation and the fact that she continued to live in the unfashionable western suburbs:

> I was in … a place that was obviously so socio-economically way out of my grasp to start with … And she kept trying to mould me into her little protégé and told me that I had to move out of my house… Find a nice law student who lived in the inner city to live with.

The cultural invigilation extended to her choice of food for lunch:

> I would bring a ham, cheese and tomato sandwich for lunch and a chocolate bar. She told me that I shouldn't be eating the bread because of the lecithin and the gluten in it, that ham is being made of pigs over here and I should only eat organic products. So she started making food for me at lunch.

Nada grew increasingly resistant to this sort of cultural makeover and to the compromises required for social mobility.

> She was really angry that I still spoke to my friends. Because when she left [her home town], which was the 'hole of holes' apparently, she didn't speak to any of her friends, and that's how she made it. So I have to do the same thing to make it like her. And I hadn't done it. And I said to her: 'To a certain degree I can't swallow changing that much of myself.'

Tanja's tribulations

Tanja, in her mid-twenties, an outgoing and confident young woman, grew up in western Sydney. A creative youth, and a talented dancer, she earned money teaching dance to young children. Her parents, both from working-class families, had both trained to be teachers on state scholarships. Her mother was a second-generation Italian migrant, and worked in a primary school during Tanja's childhood, while her father was the primary carer for his daughters. After she left school, she heard from a cousin, who was working for a fashion-industry company, that there was a job vacancy, and Tanja applied and was successful:

> [A] lot of … opportunities seem to fall in my lap, touch wood, so if something comes along … I am not the sort of person to say 'oh no no I am doing this', I will just take it. That is why I have done so many

things. … Because I think you never know what is around the corner and what if you don't dip your toe [in].

Like Nada, Tanja described a moment of magical opportunity, a happy tendency for things to just fall 'in her lap'. She told us that she is adventurous and ready to dip 'a toe in the water' rather than pursuing a predetermined course. This breezy flexibility, readiness to seize a lucky opportunity and to parlay creative skills in new directions accords with the sort of qualities that neo-liberalism requires of workers. By contrast, the strategic, career-oriented worker is less biddable, more singular of ambition.

At first, Tanja was thrilled by the job ('It was a lot of work but it was exciting and I did love the job.') and seduced by the glamorous world into which it catapulted her. She was involved in media work, connecting fashion designers to journalists, particularly from magazines. Employed for three years, she took a course in public relations and marketing with a view to building a career. But marking herself as worthy of career advancement required more than just hard work, skill and study. The presentation of self was at least as important (Goffman, 1959):

> Yeah, yeah just I mean a lot of the girls didn't know where you were from but they could tell where you were … they had the … Louis Vuitton bags and that sort of thing. … I didn't wear any label sort of clothing.

Tanja's refusal to participate in this symbolic realm by spending money on expensive clothes ('Obviously I couldn't afford to pay for things like that.') marked her as an outsider. Something about the job created tensions with her parents at home:

> I would come home and I would speak to my mum how I would be spoken to at work, and she would be like don't you speak to me like that, like I would just be a little bit cocky I think. … I was getting a little bit too big for my boots.

Tanja eventually became disillusioned with the competitive, privileged and shallow social relations of the fashion industry. ('It was just all about the clothes and I started to see how superficial it was.') She could see how elite connections opened doors that would never be opened to her:

> There are lots of people in the industry that work for nothing. Like we had a girl that came and assisted me at a busy time and she came from a really wealthy family and she just didn't have anything to do, so she just

came and worked with us … my boss would hire them because it was such and such's sister's friend and 'Oh, she is a lovely girl.'

While such young women often had little ambition or talent, they were valued and provided with opportunities that were not available to Tanja:

I would go to fashion shows and things and followed [my boss] around but … some of the girls would get seats in the front row … and we would be running around at the [back] … it would have been nice to be able to see you know to watch the show, or see part of it.

When her boss became pregnant, Tanja and her cousin were left with the major responsibility of running the business's day-to-day affairs for a time. But they were not completely trusted:

[S]he couldn't come in so she wanted us to write down everything we did and she would go through it … like really minute little things, she wanted to know every single thing that we had done in the day … all this pressure to do these work reports instead of getting stuff done.

Tanja attributed this lack of trust to her being an outsider. In addition to the dawning awareness of the informal, class-based hierarchies, Tanja could see that a fashion career would require her to become restless, mobile and tactical, never being prepared to settle in one job for too long (we look into this further in Chapter 6). She eventually found the demands of the job too onerous:

I just realized that it wasn't what I wanted to do and the pressure and the hours, the hours that you worked that you didn't get paid for, I wasn't enjoying myself anymore, it was just becoming – not difficult, it wasn't difficult work, but I was like, 'This isn't my life.' … I wasn't let out of the office a lot either, like we didn't have she didn't give us lunch proper lunch breaks like we worked and ate at the same like lunch on the computer, didn't get out of the office very much because there was always, she needed more staff but she was too tight to hire more.

Such intense demands are typical of most work in creative industries (Gill, 2008, 2009). The expectation that workers work unpaid overtime, sacrificing family and personal life, has led to what Adkins (1999) has called a re-traditionalization of gender relations in the new economy. While men are often inclined to partici-pate in such a work culture, women are not. Tanja quit her job and her public-relations course at college and abandoned plans for a career in fashion. When we interviewed her she was training to be a primary-school teacher.

Locked Out of the Social Factory: The Network and the Postmodern Career

> The metropolis is to the multitude what the factory was to the industrial working class. The factory constituted in the previous era the primary site and posed the conditions for three central activities of the industrial working class: its production; its internal encounters and organization; and its expressions of antagonism and rebellion. The contemporary productive activities of the multitude, however, overflow the factory walls to permeate the entire metropolis, and in the process the qualities and potential of those activities are transformed fundamentally.
>
> Michael Hardt and Antonio Negri, *Commonwealth*

The factory, the works and the mill were an imposing presence on the industrial urban landscape, but the social factory, as Hardt and Negri describe it, is more abstract, its shape more difficult to fathom. It is comprised of a diffuse network of new-economy freelancers, sole traders and small companies. And despite the idea that the internet makes propinquity less important to economic activity, such activity tends to form into urban clusters. Those who aspire to work in these fields must access the the informal networks through which most jobs are allocated. Unless they can get access to industry gatekeepers – the agents and brokers of the new economy – they will get nowhere, regardless of how hard they work, or how eager and talented they are. The remarkable rise of co-work centres in big cities, where freelancers rent office space, often expensively, demonstrates the limitation of the idea of mixing residential space and workspace, and the desire for opportunities for building contacts. These places provide freelancers with many of the facilities of an office – as well as, often, free coffee and food – but a major function is to provide opportunities to meet other freelancers. While public libraries can also serve as de facto workspaces, as can cafes (or 'coffices', as they have been termed), you are less likely to make contact with people in similar situations than you are in formal co-work spaces. In this section we will look more closely at the idea of the network and the practice of networking.

In the Great Depression, unemployed workers would gather in the early morning outside the factories and wharves in the desperate search for work. When the foreman came out to pick the casual day labourers, men would clamour to be among the chosen few. Most went home to hungry families with no money. The spectacle of workers climbing over each others' backs to compete for scraps of paid work is burned deep into the collective memory of the labour movement. It underpinned campaigns for job security in the second half of the twentieth century and for unemployment benefits for the victims of downturns in the business cycle. By the sixties, with near full employment, the conditions that had created misery of the 1930s seemed to be gone. But today, half a century on, workers are once again fighting for scarce work. In the new economy, the rise of unorthodox forms of employment – casual work contracts, freelancing, subcontracting and unpaid internships – have replaced Fordism's job security.

Blogger Raphael Pope-Sussman (2012) wrote that 'A friend of mine spent one day of his internship assembling an Ikea desk in his boss's bedroom. I once saw a posting on Craigslist for an "ice-cream intern." The ice-cream shop wanted someone to scoop ice cream for no pay.'

This is nowhere more apparent than in the creative industries, where in most fields the supply of labour greatly outstrips demand. Unlike those who gathered at the daily call-up in the thirties, today's reserve army of creative workers is hidden and dispersed. For sure, they are not so desperate as the unemployed of the Great Depression, because most live in and around large cities where low-paid and insecure day jobs can usually be found in shops, bars or cafes. Nevertheless, they are unfulfilled, with little chance to practice and be paid for the skills they spent years training to develop. The barista in your local cafe might also be a graduate in fine arts, deriving very little creative satisfaction from describing floral designs in the froth on the top of your morning coffee. The only opportunity the out-of-work actor gets to pull on the mask of performance is at a reception desk while dealing with irate customers. Creatives are legion in global cities. They are the call-centre workers who try to sell you life insurance in an unwanted Friday evening phone call; they are the theatre-box-office ticket sellers with unusually polished customer service skills; they are the smart young things helping you to choose an outfit in the high street clothing outlet. They have a film script tucked away out the back, or an idea for a creative start-up that just requires some venture capital, or just an ingénue's eagerness to perform their talents. Most will have presented their work publicly – a screening, funding pitch, performance or exhibition –and received encouragement for their efforts. But critical praise doesn't pay the rent on the tiny room in an inner-city share house, or for the overpriced groceries in the shops in the 'groovy neighbourhood' in which they struggle to live. For now, they have to tread water as best they can until the break comes along.

By contrast with the foreman standing on a box picking out the lucky few, the creative gatekeepers are less visible. The creative aspirants can never been completely sure who has the power to give them a break. Life's a pitch (Gill, 2010) and you can never be sure who is worth pitching to. In the creative economy, where work is often short term and project based, informal networks operate as sources of information and opportunities. But the powerful creative networks are elusive and difficult to break into. They are what Maffesoli (1995) termed neo-tribal, assembling in public, outside of workspaces only occasionally and fleetingly. So the aspirant has to track down and make contact with key network members, otherwise they will simply dissolve back into the crowd where they are virtually impossible to spot. If in the past dress codes marked vocational hierarchies, today everyone is informal: the ubiquitous t-shirt and jeans serve as camouflage and the powerful are indistinguishable from the aspirants. So the latter must develop the skill of hunting down the former at social gatherings. They must work the room for all it is worth, decoding people quickly, making snap judgements about their contact value and how much they can enhance their career prospects.

Middle-aged men are usually a good bet. A few years ago, at the opening of a Japanese film festival, a young woman approached George with exaggerated familiarity, a modus operandi typical of middle-class creative youngsters on the make. After a couple of minutes, during which she was effusive and charming, George told her he was an academic. Her face went blank. She turned on her heel and made off into the crowd, without so much as a parting pleasantry or a backward glance. He was not a critic, a producer or industry executive, and therefore not worth spending another precious minute with. She headed off else-where, handing out cards like a blackjack dealer, circulating like a speed dater through the room. It was easy to admire her chutzpah, but also easy to pity her predicament. Here she was, a wannabe in a room full of people she didn't know and with the clock ticking: a bundle of unfulfilled potential in search of an outlet.

There is a hidden trope that governs this exchange: the belief that fame and the big break could emerge from one chance encounter with a stranger. In many respects, as we noted in the previous chapter, this is the romance narrative mutated by late modernity. Cities filled with strangers have long drawn young people seeking to change their lives, to remake themselves socially and culturally. What drove their metropolitan meanderings were the romantic and erotic possi-bilities that crowds of strangers hint at. Out there, amidst the teeming multitude, is someone who could change your life, the beautiful or handsome stranger, the groovy new friend who can initiate you into bohemia. But the creative flâneurs are not just seeking love in the metropolitan crowd; they are desperate to find a foothold for their creative career. There is a paradox at the heart of the network society: we have sold creative fulfilment to young people, yet we give them no maps to consummate their vocational ambitions – creativity is everywhere, yet its outlets are more diffuse, its audiences more fickle and elusive and its rewards less and less tangible. In the city, everywhere seems pregnant with possibility and yet nowhere can it be clearly made out. So it's desirable to stay as close to the creative clusters, the cool, highly caffeinated 24/7 hipster spaces in which start-ups are crammed in the warehouse conversion and the odour of single-origin lattes waft out from cafes that look like soup kitchens.

The Film-makers' Network

The setting is a fashionable pub in Surry Hills, the epicentre of Sydney's hipster boho scene and the creative economy hub. Funky deep-house music plays in the background as customers recline on retro lounges decorated with old, boldly coloured cushions. Candlelight illuminates the vintage décor. The trendy inner-city crowd are sipping their mid-week wine and boutique beer – Panama hats and long scarves, chatting and thumbing their smartphones. The bar staff – young and effortlessly cool – wear the latest haircuts, beards, tattoos and designer jeans. They spin drinking glasses on their hands and pour long shots into short glasses from expensive spirit bottles.

It is here that the monthly meetings of the Film-makers' Network (FN) are held. The attendance averages around 25, with a core of regulars. Unlike guilds or professional networks, you need no professional accreditation or even industry work experience to belong. There are no expensive joining fees. The FN is an informal networking group populated mainly by aspirants rather than established professionals. The meeting begins with casting and crew calls, including calls for volunteers for short films, and invitations for members to speak briefly about their projects, including script developments. Those lucky enough to get some paid work will talk to the group about their achievements and urge members to attend shows, film screenings and performances. The meetings are structured but not particularly formal: people order drinks and dinner, move around, come and go as they choose.

Then a guest speaker – someone with industry standing – will be given the floor for an hour, at the end of which they take questions. This allows the more confident in the audience to display their knowledge and chutzpah. But sometimes things fall flat. On one occasion, the guest speaker told a story about working on a film and invited group members to talk about similar experiences, only to be met with a blank silence. FN members are mostly amateurs or aspirants, not professional film-makers, and most lack the experience on which to base such stories. After question time, the meeting wraps up, with people breaking off and starting their own conversations and others lining up for the chance to talk with the speaker.

At the end of one meeting, we observe a young woman handing out her business card to anyone who would take one – twice to Pariece. She tells her she is an aspiring screenwriter, but works during the day as a receptionist. She attends FN meetings regularly, volunteers for the organization and for roles in short films. When Pariece explains that she is a researcher and would be unable to help her find work, the young woman insists on giving her a card anyway, in case one day she can. Another aspirant, who recently arrived in Sydney from New Zealand, took a more targeted approach. She circulated through the crowd, quizzing people about their skills, work experience and future plans. She introduced herself to Pariece, but after discovering she was a researcher, quickly went off in search of more powerful contacts.

The convenor of the FN tries to attract influential people, both to strengthen the group's reputation but also to bolster his own networks. Like other group members, he is on the fringes of the industry, but his 'day job' as a medical specialist is lucrative and comfortably subsidises his creative ambitions. He has written a feature film by drawing upon his hospital experience (describing it as a 'modern-day version of MASH') but has been unable to find financial backers.

The FN is a broad network that includes a variety of the film-industry precariat: from actors and scriptwriters to directors and technical workers. The convenor tells us that 'It's an educational and networking forum, so the more diversity the better.' The group's Facebook page shows that it has nearly 2,500 members, although only a few are active – people move on, they become dormant, modify their ambitions. Access to the 'Red Folder', which lists available cast and crew and includes biographies and headshots of actors, is restricted to financial members, as are special events like script-writing workshops. Those who pay subscriptions also receive discounts at affiliated service providers such as film schools and consultancy and production firms. Most members have day jobs in bars, cafes or shops, although some have started their own small production companies. Many are tentative about their creative identities: Jessica (20) does film-making 'on the side' while Jimmy (50) describes it as a 'second career'. The lack of experience weighs heavily on such people.

Most FN members cannot afford to live in or around Surry Hills, where the meetings are held, because even the smallest, most rundown apartment is beyond their means. But ironically, this is the locale in which creative enterprises are most densely concentrated with the most active networks. For those with little industry work experience, the opportunity to come together once a month to discuss the craft of film-making allows them to feel part of the inner-city scene. Various researchers of gentrification (Lloyd, 2010; Zukin, 1989) have shown that when struggling artists/bohemians move into a rundown urban area, they can help make it trendy and attractive. This leads to increasingly high rents and land values. Only those who are entrepreneurially successful – able to make a profit from their creative activity – can survive the process of gentrification. The penniless bohemians are long since banished to the next frontier, where they will eventually suffer the same fate.

Surry Hills is a textbook example of this process. For much of its history it was a district of great poverty, home to one of Sydney's most notorious slums, Frog Hollow. Ruth Park wrote in her 1940s novel *The Harp in the South* that the houses of Surry Hills smelled of 'leaking gas and rats' and that most of Sydney associated the area with 'brothels, razor gangs, tenements and fried fish shops'. In the 1980s, the middle classes began to buy up and renovate terrace houses (once derided as slums).[2] The streetscapes now betray the area's hipster identity, with outlets typical of creative hubs throughout the Western world: galleries, cafes and bars selling artisan brews, organic grocers, a variety of ethnic restaurants, book and antique shops and emporia of vintage clothing or furniture. It is the sort of urbane, cultural space that Florida suggests contributes to the 'experiential life' to which people gravitate in order to 'reinforce their identities as creative people' (Florida, 2003, p. 166).

By meeting in Surry Hills, with its edgy cultural and subcultural associations, FN members can reinforce their creative identities. At one meeting a young man expressed his approval at the fact that a scheduled script-development workshop had been moved from Bondi, where it was originally located, and which houses a very different subcultural scene ('the home of surfers', he pointed out) to Surry Hills ('the home of film-makers'). The setting is important to those with limited film-making experience, because they feel they are part of the scene. The pub and the network are surrogates for the studio and the work group. The gathering provides members with institutional affirmation for their vocational aspirations, giving some solidity to their professional aspirations.

The annual short-film festival brings dormant FN members out of the woodwork and attracts new ones. Some established film-makers participate in the event, which is held in an art-deco cinema in Sydney's eastern suburbs, esteemed by the local film-making community, and where art-house film premieres are sometimes held. Such a venue has the cachet needed by the FN to attract new members, other film-makers and a wider, general audience.

Before the films are shown, people gather for drinks in the bar. It feels like a highly charged networking event, with eyes darting around the room as network members try to spot famous faces. Eventually we are ushered to our seats and welcomed by the MC, who then introduces the organizers, judges and the directors of the seven finalist films. This year, no FN member made the shortlist – such was the competition from people outside the network. But the festival received some media coverage, and the organizers engaged a television personality and cameraperson to move amongst the crowd doing vox pops. They made an effort to mimic the familiar Hollywood-style red carpet events to accentuate the sense that the festival was professionally important.

---

2 A report published in 2013 found that Surry Hills was the centre of the Sydney's creative industries, particularly design and media (www.sgsep.com.au/news/valuing-australias-creative-industries-report-released-/). The 'Catch and Release' research project undertaken by Chris Gibson and Chris Brennan Horley, researchers from the University of Wollongong (http://gpscreate.com/case-studies/catch_and_release//), tracked the movements of 14 creative-industry workers over two weeks and found Surry Hills to be their most frequented district.

The winner was announced at the after-party, where there was the opportunity to mingle. But many network members stood around the edges of the room nursing their drinks like nervous teenagers at the school dance, intimidated by the presence of more experienced film-makers and lacking the confidence to work the room. The experience of feeling inadequate and unworthy of the company at such events is very typical of creative aspirants. As a music production student interviewee declared in frustrated exasperation, 'It's all about who you know and I don't know shit!'

The organizers were less diffident about speaking to strangers but even they had appeared more at home in the familiar surrounds of regular FN meetings. So the film festival was a double-edged sword: it presented the sense that important contacts could be made but it also demonstrated that the FN was not a real industry network. It took the presence of professionals to reinforce their sense of membership in the creative-reserve army of people on the precarious fringes of an exclusive industry. The group seeks to build what network theorists call 'bridging capital' (Gitell and Vidal, 1998), to provide aspirants with bridges from the industry's margins to its centre, but it has only limited success in this ambition.

Trainees in the film and television industry learn that networks are crucial to future employment prospects, as most work is project-based and performed by freelancers (Blair, 2001, 2003; Christopherson, 2008). Most work is allocated informally and, as McRobbie writes, 'The conventions associated with the traditional CV and the job application process are nothing short of overturned in the network culture' (2002b, p. 527). But the network is a volatile structure, by contrast with the fixed community of practice based in established workplaces (Lave and Wenger, 1991). It is not solid and tangible despite the fact that mapping networks and tracing their operation has become an academic sub-discipline – the purpose of networking is to embellish and even to transcend existing networks. It is a linguistic irony that the verb 'to network' has the effect of undermining the noun, the network. Organizations like the FN are only useful insofar as they involve some turnover in personnel – fresh faces at meetings who offer hope of broader horizons. It is more useful to be a member of a sparser network with well-positioned individuals who offer diverse information than it is to be part of a large network of redundant contacts connected to the same people and who offer the same information. As Blair (2003, 2009) affirms, it is not so much the density (or size) of the network that is important but the status of the people within it.

Despite the collaborative rhetoric that characterizes FN meetings, the short supply of work can encourage network members to be competitive, individualistic and opportunistic. Colleagues and/or coworkers are also competitors and there is a compulsion for people to protect or preserve their resources, information and occupational opportunity. Bob, an FN member, recalled that when he was experiencing financial hardship he chose not to share information about upcoming jobs with friends, colleagues or network members. He understood that this was ethically dubious but observed that 'You do what you gotta do.' Such opportunism is understandable in competitive, project-based labour markets but it can destabilize networks and compromise friendships and undermine solidarities.

Come Help Out. No, Don't Bother …

Many of those in creative-training courses told us that they hoped their teachers and even fellow students might open doors for them. McRobbie argues that, in the networked society, the university assumes much larger importance in shoehorning people into careers. 'Top or "branded" universities promise graduates better access to big companies seeking to outsource creative work, and the same holds true for appointments with venture capitalists' (2002b, p. 527). She also writes that professional networks have their genesis in the social/'party' networks that form part of undergraduate life:

> Universities and colleges become key sites for developing the social skills for the network (once again often as party organizer), so, for [those] who at present do not enjoy three years of higher education, this is a further absence of opportunity. (It is also unlikely that mature students who are concentrated in poorer universities are in the position to immerse themselves in the hedonistic and expensive culture of networking.). (2002b, p. 527)

Thus the Oxbridge relations of patronage, so despised by the advocates of meritocracy, reassert themselves in smoothing access to the informal labour markets of the new economy. Contrary to the principles of social democracy, the old school networks are again becoming important, whether they are formed in the venerable institutions of higher learning, or in the new universities in which much creative training takes place. Post-school education institutions, like networks, can be complex and variegated spaces of solidarity and competition, of friendship and rivalry. Film schools provide resources and group activities to help initiate relationships. However, it is the informal relations that are established between students that enable networks to flourish, and it is the potential mentorship provided by teachers that also contributes to network expansion and transcendence.

Those who study at college rather than university may find their access to networks more limited. David, who studied film in a government technical college, struck up a friendship with his teacher, Alan, whom David recalled warmed to his enthusiasm and offered him an opportunity to get some work experience:

> He was saying 'Yeah, man, come down some time, I'm happy to help you.' So anyway, I got down there and it was going well and then he was saying, 'If you're really interested we're hopefully going to be filming the Big Top concert.' … I thought, this is pretty cool, but unfortunately he rang me saying that it had been kinda cancelled and that even though they would be filming, they couldn't bring me along. I was a bit annoyed because I kinda thought, how come you couldn't, I'd be there in a flash. So from then on I didn't really have any more contact with him, but I still kept making my movie.

Like many of those from less privileged backgrounds, with families who are remote from the cultural scenes, David was trying to get a foot in the door, but was vulnerable to the capricious withdrawal of an offer. The informal and improvised character of film projects means that so many opportunities are allocated by word-of-mouth and it is easy to break promises in open networks, where contacts are diffuse and people expendable, even those who are offering to work for nothing. The contrast with training in blue-collar settings is clear: an employer would have been obliged to provide the hands-on experience to an apprentice but the lack of secure work means that graduates struggle for opportunities to practice skills that might become stale.

Many proponents of the new economy are optimistic about networks and project-based work (Leadbeater, 1999), seeing their ephemeral and fluid nature as allowing opportunities they would not otherwise be able to achieve where long-term employees of companies perform most of the work. But others recognize how powerful networks can operate to exclude people with talent. Blair observed that what she calls semi-permanent work groups perform much work in the film industry, and that these groups can work to exclude those seen as a threat or a disruption to established workers (Blair, 2001, 2003). The networks in which freelance workers in film and television come together are profoundly inegalitarian (Blair, 2003, p. 691).

Jack, a film school graduate, worked in a cafe known for being a haunt of actors and producers and each day took his film script to work in a satchel just on the off chance that he might be able to show it to someone with influence. One day, he got chatting with a minor celebrity who had enjoyed a measure of fame and some Hollywood work earlier in his career but who had remained a jobbing actor:

I cracked and said, 'What's it like working with [cult director] ... and he went on for about half an hour about how wonderful it was and he said, 'Oh, you're a film-maker, are you?' And I said I was working on a short film. I showed him the script and he said, 'Can I be in it?' And I said, 'Yeah alright, you're in.' And the girl who instigated the whole thing [the film project] wanted a meeting with him and she was nervous about meeting him, you know he's just a guy ... it turns out that he texted me a week before shooting saying he couldn't do it and they wanted him a week early [for another project] so I was yeah, no worries, so we got a different actor and [the girl] got stressed and it was never made because she [abandoned] the film.

This narrative illustrates how informal power operates in the film and television industry network (Blair, 2001, 2003). Actors need to keep working to stay credible and this actor agreed to appear in this student film to fill the gaps in his schedule. He engaged in the common practice of stacking his diary, making commitments he could easily relinquish if something better came along. While work on a student film is pro bono, it can nevertheless provide established actors with street cred. For the student film-makers the stakes were higher. The ability to attract a 'star' to their unpaid, amateur production gave them hope that it might lead to professional work later on and at least connect them to larger networks. It cost the actor very little to renege on his promise to the students, but they suffered disappointment and embarrassment, and this led them to abandon the film.

Jack's narrative also illustrates how, in a world of project-based work, professional identity claims are simultaneously plausible and precarious. Where once your ability to claim an occupational status rested entirely on whether or not you had a steady job in that field, now in creative fields even experienced professionals are unemployed for a good part of the year. You need not necessarily be currently employed in order to be part of the guild. The illusion of comradeship masks the hierarchies that exist in creative industries composed of freelancers. To be asked by a famous actor, 'Oh you're a film-maker, are you?' and then to have interest shown in his work, provides Jack with a powerful affirmation of his aspirations, a confirmation that they live in the same world. They discuss the intricacies of a cult-classic film and talk as equals about a legendary Hollywood director. Jack tells us that the actor is 'just a guy', but the relationships between them are profoundly unequal. This becomes apparent when the actor withdraws and Jack plays down his disappointment: 'I was yeah, no worries.' He tries to save face, but his powerlessness is confirmed when his partner disbands the film project as an implicit consequence of this withdrawal.

Conclusion

Youth has long been synonymous with the quest for independence, for liberation from parental and communal constraints and expectations. This independence is marked out in cultural terms. As traditional sources of employment
decline, and the discourse of creative economic renewal intensifies, so increasing numbers of young people have sought to build careers on their cultural
interests. But creative aspirants from poor areas – suburban or provincial –
generally feel the need to leave their homes in order to succeed. In Australia,
the geography of aspiration reverses the pattern of the mid-twentieth century,
when working people moved out to the suburbs in search of social mobility.
Instead of moving out to the detached house, the car, the consumer goods and
the nuclear family, our subjects move inwards, towards what they see as the
social and cultural centres.[3] But in a world where patterns of taste/consump-
tion are more complex and difficult to map onto class structures, the cultural
challenges associated with social mobility are formidable.[4] Leon described the
neo-tribal journey: the quest to track down the micro-scenes to which he felt
he belonged and that could liberate him from random suburban clustering.
John recalled his wish to trade the bland cultural consumption of the suburbs,
to live in a place more congenial to writing and performing original music.
Such journeys are a particularly contemporary vision, combining life and art,
work and play. The pursuit of the creative vocation involves rolling private into
public, hobby into work, friendship groups into career networks (McRobbie,
1993). But moving from subculture to career is complex and hazardous.

    The modern career relied on relatively stable forms of capital – credentials,
references from past employers, a stock of demonstrable skills, recognizable
scripts for performing career accomplishments. In the highly volatile circumstances of the new economy, the postmodern career is a different game. It is
up to the worker to join the career dots, and to make the connections between
the work experiences and life projects. There are fewer rules and so much
more rests on your ability to talk the talk, to give a plausible career narrative.
But the principal challenge is to decide when, where and to whom to tell this
story – to track down the people who know where the work is and can decide
who gets it. Their networks mostly convene informally in public places and

---

3 Ironically, though, the places that more genuinely signify the class divide, where those
   with real wealth and power reside, were barely even on the radar of most of those we
   interviewed.
4 We note the complex picture revealed in Bennett et al.'s (1999) survey of contemporary
   cultural consumption and distinction/taste, and the contrast offered with Bourdieu's
   (1984) landmark study of class patterning.

so are elusive, and attempts to formalize them, such as with the FN, rarely work in a way that reproduces opportunity. And in the 'no-collar' culture of creative industries, the mise-en-scène and the props for performing vocational worthiness are not clearly agreed upon. The most powerful person in the industry might be the person in the room that is dressed most informally. Creative aspirants must find a way of making progress in a world where the source of opportunity is camouflaged and dispersed. Such people will often tell stories of peers for whom a chance meeting with a powerful stranger profoundly reshaped their lives. But narratives like these are symptomatic of how profoundly powerless and vulnerable creative aspirants are, and how, under new capitalism, career advancement is far from meritocratic. In the new world, contacts and cool trump talent and hard work every time. By contrast with Leon's and John's subcultural journeys, those of Nada and Tanja were driven by the excitement at the prospect of glamorous creative work in hip districts of Sydney. However, each experienced scrutiny and pressure, cultural judgement and the sense of being unworthy and marginal. They were unwilling to dress/present themselves in the manner expected of young career aspirants. When they became aware of what the metropolitan journey entailed, they withdrew and recalibrated their ambitions in less precarious and competitive directions.

Chapter 4

DO GIVE UP YOUR DAY JOB

Introduction

As we have seen, the oversupply of creative labour has produced a creative underclass (or 'reserve army' in Marx's terms), most members of which must find alternative sources of income to tide them over in down times. Those without savings or family money have to find 'day jobs' – usually part-time work flexible enough to allow them to keep their creative ambitions alive. In recent history, there has been a growth in service-sector work, mostly in retail and hospitality. American retailer Walmart has the largest workforce of any private company in the world, and in Australia two supermarket chains are the largest employers. 'McJobs' with such employers can help creative aspirants to mitigate the effects of un/underemployment. In metropolitan centres in the West, most of those who work in bars, shops, cafes and call centres have larger aspirations. The popular assumption is that these are youth jobs: something to sustain you in the transition to the more steady career of adulthood. (Although as Weissman, 2012, has argued, this is not the case – not in the United States, at least.) So they are generally lower paid and more precarious than other sources of employment. However, as we have seen, youth transitions in the West are longer and more fraught today than in the post-war period when full-time employment was more plentiful.[1] Most of our interviewees spoke of the day job as a necessary evil, something that allowed them to tread water while waiting for real life to begin. It also allows them to maintain the purity of an artistic identity, to hold at bay the point at which they are required to compromise, to parlay their creative skills into some labour-market niche, or commercial expression. But if aspirants tread water for too long they risk the creeping sense that the day job will come to define them. This chapter will deal with the complicated and ambivalent relationship that creative aspirants have to their day jobs.

The rise of precarious work is well documented (Beck, 2000; Campbell, 2004; Standing, 2011), and resisting 'precarity' has informed the actions of social movements in different parts of the world – the indignados in Spain, the Saint Precariat movement in Italy, and the Occupy movement in various parts of the world. Campbell (2004) compared the rise of temporary employees as a proportion of the overall workforce in various countries between 1983 and 2002. He found that in France it rose from 3.3 to 14.1 per cent, in the Netherlands from 5.8 to 14.3 per cent and in Spain from 15.7 to 31.2 per cent. In Australia, Burgess et al. (2008, p. 165) calculated that there has been an increase in casual employees as a proportion of all of those in employment from 15.8 per cent in 1984 to 26.9 per cent in 2006. Precarious work has increased across the workforce, including in established professions (Chan and Tweedie, 2015), and is particularly concentrated amongst young and female workers (Burgess et al., 2008, p. 166). However, in recent history, the increase in the proportion of men employed in casual and other precarious forms of employment outstrips the growth amongst women employees. In Britain, where temporary employment is less common, the current problem is the very rapid growth in 'zero-hour contracts' – under which employers are not obliged to supply their workers with any paid hours during the working week. Those employed under this arrangement rose from 697,000 in 2014 to 744,000 in 2015 at a time when employment growth was relatively flat, from 2 per cent to 2.4 per cent of the workforce (UK Office of National Statistics, 2015).

---

1 In Australia there has been a steady rise in underemployment – from around 800,000 workers in 2010 to around one million five years later (ABS, 2015). In Britain those in this category represent 5.9 per cent of the workforce (Blanchflower, 2015).

The wider debates on non-standard employment revolve around whether it is designed simply to allow companies greater workforce flexibility (to cut hours when business is slack) and to relinquish obligations they have to long-term employees (Campbell, 2001, 2010) – the sick and recreation leave, contributions to pensions and so forth – or whether it provides some reciprocal advantage to employees. This latter perspective states that workers too can benefit from such flexibility, allowing them to cope with the fluctuating demands on their time arising from the erratic work patterns of the postmodern career. While it is certainly true that non-standard forms of employment need not be any more flexible than standard employment,[2] creative aspirants tend to look for those employers who can accommodate erratic work patterns – working full time some weeks and other weeks not available at all. Creative work patterns can be unpredictable and difficult to manage, making it difficult to plan ahead. Work opportunities can appear with very little warning, particularly for those who operate on a freelance/short-contract basis, with the just-in-time, word-of-mouth, improvised character of creative projects.

Students in creative/performing-arts courses are now often taught that they should not become too attached to their day jobs because they might have to jettison them at the drop of a hat – when a job comes along that takes them off for a month or two, an intensive period of rehearsals and performances that takes all their time. It is difficult to plan too far ahead when the rhythms of working life are so uncertain. At any moment you could be called for an audition (or, for other creative workers, perhaps a meeting with a client or funding body to pitch your creative ideas) and if you've committed to a shift in a restaurant or bar you just have to call in sick or tell them you can't make it. You risk angering the employer/supervisor and you might be sacked on the spot. And you may have to undertake the sort of juggling work associated with being 'flexible', like organizing for someone to cover the shift that you have committed to, or been rostered for. But aspirants are told that if they want a creative career they have to make sacrifices. There will always be service jobs for confident young people, so don't miss the opportunity to do work you are trained for.

This advice/direction encapsulates the *drop-everything syndrome* that is at the heart of the idea of the creative career. Labour markets are structured not just around precariousness but also around improvised and last-minute creative processes. The just-in-time worker must exist in a state of perpetual readiness, convinced that the big break is just over the horizon and ready to trade security for flexibility. And ideally the creative career grows to the point where it is

2 Indeed, in Australia, there is evidence that casual employment may in fact provide less flexibility than standard employment (ABS, 2009).

eventually possible to abandon the day job. But as we shall see, this is often not the case: for those who are paid little or nothing for their creative labour, day jobs are no longer day jobs. In the case studies below we will consider how the creative aspirants' sense of vocational abeyance and potential shapes the way they view their day jobs.

Day-Job Case Studies

Hardworn Roger

Roger, in his mid-twenties, is in a hip-hop band that he started with old friends from high school. He exemplifies the early-career portfolio creative worker. Ambitious to record and perform, he also runs a small event management company, which has had a couple of contracts, but does not provide enough to live on. So his most reliable source of income is working in a chain hardware store, the kind that has branches scattered across the big-box retail parks throughout suburban Australia. He has held the job on and off for a decade and at the time we interviewed him performed a minor supervisory role, but has declined opportunities to move up the managerial hierarchy. He tells us that he likes the informality of the workplace, its lack of a rigid dress code, or the sort of monitoring and direction experienced by others who work in shops and restaurants. Roger admits that the work is not particularly demanding and that the people he supervises have the same 'vibe':

> Obviously your appearance isn't a huge thing as long as you get in there, do your job and pretty much do everything as required. The people there are a lot cooler. I get on with them a lot better, I know what I am doing down there.

Roger describes what he sees as a sort of tacit agreement with the company under which he can take time out when working on creative projects but he doesn't actually resign the job and can backtrack when he needs to.

> So when I left there I didn't quit … officially I was just still casual so I was still on the books, [I went for] this other job, stayed on the books, once I knew I was not liking it I called up [the DIY chain] and got more hours there.

This contrasts with the Fordist standard-employment work contract with a single employer, under which work and working life had a predictable rhythm and where incomes were relatively stable. This arrangement benefits the company, allowing it to avoid the cost of recruiting and training, and the risk that new employees may not work out. Roger can pick up where he left off, needs no extra training, but is also aware of how precarious his situation is. With high youth unemployment and the possibility that economic recession will reduce demand for workers, his income can disappear at any moment.

After leaving school, Roger considered taking on a trade apprenticeship but now feels that he has passed the age where this is economically viable:

> Obviously if you don't start that when you are kind of 16 or 17 you have kind of wasted the opportunity, because who wants to go back to eight dollars an hour when you are 23 so the whole tradesman kind of apprenticeship thing doesn't really work kind of once you get past that.

Now in his retail work he deals with tradespeople and home handypeople, an experience that resonates with his vaguely knockabout blue-collar masculinity: 'I am more of an active person – either sport, music, more of a hands-on person.' Although his father had a sedentary job, Roger wanted to avoid that fate. His day-job narrative is typical of that of many creative young people who have incorporated the routine, precarious casual job into their sense of self. They have no wish to return to Fordist routine, to commit to the steady job, for this would cramp their style, compromise their individuality and autonomy, and undermine their artistic and rebellious identity.

Roger's band has yet to make it, but he tells us he sees it as a long game, and will keep his options open. He appears easy with his situation but this may be just bravado. Several young men we interviewed had a similar disposition, unwilling to concede to self-doubt or frustrated ambition. You juggle the various parts of the portfolio and even if nothing ever completely comes to the boil, in your twenties you must give the appearance of being in charge of your own destiny. But this cannot be the case forever; as some of their peers acquire the hallmarks of social maturity – house, relationship, better incomes – they risk experiencing the sense of being left behind. It is wrong to see people like Roger just as victims of oppressive social change of the erosion of incomes and job security. However, while it is important to recognize their agency in improvising a set of work relations that keep them afloat, it is indeed a very limited form of agency involving a good deal of youthful bluff.

Neil on the rebound

We met Neil in Chapter 2, a twenty-seven-year-old of middle-class background who took up music at high school. He described becoming the token 'school rebel', and recalled his ostentatious shows of subcultural resistance with pride. Some of his teachers and fellow students liked him and indulged his eccentricity, but he had no interest in study and did poorly at high school.

Conscious of his lack of credentials, he rationalizes his reluctance to study music formally:

> People would want me to do music at university and I thought the last thing I want to do ... I do music for enjoyment, not to become a music teacher or something like that. Music is a very personal thing for me and the last thing I wanted to do was go and write papers on it and you know instruct it and demystify it you know and studying an art like that just didn't appeal to me.

He embraces a bohemian, nonconformist view of his music – it is all or nothing – one that makes him ill-suited to the sort of improvised portfolio creative career. Neil refuses to treat his creative skills as abstract, transferable and marketable. Even teaching music in a formal setting compromises him:

> The stuff I enjoy about music does not exist when you are teaching a bunch of fifth graders how to play ... the theme from Aladdin or something ... knew I wasn't going to do that for the rest of my life.

By contrast with Roger, Neil briefly enjoyed some commercial musical success, and tried to give up his day job delivering pizzas. His fellow band members were also

> ... all working part-time jobs so yeah you know but then it probably started to get a little more serious ... people started putting money behind us yeah you know we got signed to a label, our debut album came out, the label you know flew us to Adelaide to record it and put us up in an apartment for a few weeks. So yeah did all that stuff.

But in the end this came to nothing much and when money was short he moved back in with his parents, 'crawled my sorry arse' back to the pizza shop and, like Roger, was given work again. While Neil was reluctant to reflect too much on the inability to make a living playing music, his narrative of day-job entrapment – of being dragged back to the drudge work that he had tried so desperately to escape – powerfully illustrates the fluctuating fortunes of the creative career.

Jerome wasn't built in a day

Jerome was not academically inclined as a child but showed an aptitude for creative expression. So his wealthy parents enrolled him in a private high school that specialized in the arts and he became interested and later trained in film-making. When we interviewed him, his first feature film, a documentary, was going into post-production stage. While this project was happening, he continued to work for a slightly upmarket pizza chain. He presents a clear contrast to Roger and Neil. The fact that his creative career is on the up means Jerome can be sanguine about his day job, confident that it is temporary. He took it on because the shop was located

> down the road from me you know so I heard they were looking for a phone person and I thought, 'Fuck I could do that a couple of nights a week have a bit of pocket money.'

He works in take away order/deliveries with a colourful range of young people, none of whom take their jobs seriously, and the friendly, jovial atmosphere of the shop makes up for the low pay/status. It is even possible to work hard in short bursts despite the job being 'meaningless'.

> I don't mind it is time off you know, if anything it makes you work a bit harder because you think ok I have got to go and do that job which is not that fun, so when I get to write and stuff I am going to really be focussed and work hard.

Jerome believes that being able to work happily in such a menial job is a mark of character but of course takes it as 'obvious' that it is temporary:

> I don't really mind like I think it is all about your attitude, obviously you don't want to do it forever but it hasn't really been a problem. Some people have an ego issue like oh man I shouldn't be sweeping floors and I guess I am lucky I just don't really have that, I don't mind sweeping floors.

His sister is a doctor and he contrasts his disordered and improvised life to hers.

> I am kind of a bit more chaotic and you know you have your ups and downs and I guess I can kind of do stuff because my schedule is a bit looser. But you know … she knows exactly what the next ten years will hold and I have got all the respect in the world for her but I just couldn't live like that.

For Jerome, the day job is a key ingredient in the unfathomable and project-based character of the creative career. He is single-minded about film-making, but is confident that his career will unfold, albeit slowly. So rather than resenting his knockabout day job, he constructs it as something of a rite of passage, a necessary component of the bohemian biography.

Adam's apples

Adam, in his mid-twenties, who went to a specialist music high school in Sydney, is another aspiring film-maker, with little experience as of yet. Both his parents worked in the industry, intermittently and precariously, as did his uncle, who enjoyed a short-lived burst of fame as a star in a famous Australian feature film of the 1970s. He shares Jerome's upbeat view of the day job:

> I can look past having a crappy job and living with not very much money, and that's what I enjoy in a weird way. It's risky; yeah, I'd enjoy financial security, but it's not something I'm always certainly going to have, so sacrifice and that's okay … remember, this was my parents' lifestyle as well.

For a long time, Adam's family lived hand to mouth: 'It wasn't unstable, it's just that some times were easier than others.' His mother made a living between acting jobs by moonlighting in call centres. His father, a former actor and sound/lighting technician, eventually sought greater stability and worked in a public service job before eventually setting up a media consulting business. So when contemplating the prospect of precarious life, Adam says, 'Remember, this was my parents' lifestyle as well.' This memory of surviving despite poverty fortifies Adam against any fear of failure. The industry networks to which he has access through family connections mean that the idea of the film career is not simply a fantasy. In the meantime, he is content to work in low-paid precarious work, so long as it is not at the frayed and exploited fringes of the 'creative industry' he aspires to work in. Adam now works selling apples at a growers' market on the weekends:

> Don't mind working a normal job. What I like about working at the market is that it's so far removed from what I want to do.… [When I was young] I worked in a video shop and it was nice and it was across the road from my house, but it's close enough to what I want to do that it was painful watching movies all day, so I'd rather have something that I'm completely removed from.

Despite being determined to write and direct feature films, he does not want to enter the industry from the bottom. 'I could get work as a sound assistant … but I'd just get bored and I don't want to end up hating the industry.' Adam is not enamoured with the copy-boy-to-media-magnate narrative, with the prospect of serving a menial apprenticeship in the hope of getting the big break at some point. He has a sense of his craft skills (Banks, 2010) as non-transferable, of a calling that is both non-negotiable and indivisible. If he cannot genuinely practice this craft he would rather sell apples.

Day job for David?

David, in his late twenties, grew up in a poor, working-class family in Sydney's western suburbs. He suffers from dyslexia and so struggled both socially and academically at school:

> I had teachers going, 'Oh, you're stupid' and 'just work it out' and putting me … in front of the class and basically going, 'Look at the town freak.' I was always in the background, walking around trying to say, 'Hey, do you wanna be my mate?'

David had wanted to leave school to work with his father, a plasterer, but when the latter suffered an industrial injury that ended his building career, David was at a loose end. He managed to finish high school, with poor grades, but was encouraged to develop his cine-literacy skills, enrolled in a college film-making course and now aspires to work in the industry. Like Adam, he had worked in a video/DVD hire shop in his teens and then later found casual work in the DVD/music section of a department store. By contrast with Adam, he was happy to sell the products of other people's creative labour even though that placed him at the margins of the industry in which he hoped eventually to find more creatively rewarding work. But the hours were irregular and, still living at home, he experienced family pressure to find a more stable source of income:

> I was pressured by mum to keep asking if there's permanent part-time [rather than casual] shifts. She wanted me to do permanent shifts and so the guy I got along pretty well with, he said, 'Yes, there's hours but in homewares' and so stupid me went okay because I didn't know if I was going to keep getting enough hours in music and DVDs. People are saying, 'Do you even like homewares?' and I'm like, 'No, I just want the get money, man.' So yeah, like I don't give two shits about a wine glass or a fry pan you know.

Unlike Adam and Jerome, David found it difficult to rise above the mundane and alienating labour he was forced to perform, perhaps because he was less confident that the job was temporary. His film-industry employment prospects were meagre and the pressure to obtain a steady wage meant that selling homewares might represent his long-term fate. The family pressure for income stability cannot be explained simply by David's class background, if class is measured in income terms. Adam had also experienced poverty in his childhood but his sense of creative resilience was based on the bohemian conviction that 'something would come up'. That means he is more open than David to the prospect of long-term instability.

Zero-hour Henry

Henry Hundreds, whom we met in Chapter 2, is, like David, from a poor family and presents a clear contrast with Adam and Jerome. He told us how an ancient-history teacher's use of a popular film in his teaching fuelled his interest in film and led him to enrol in a college film course after he left school. But despite his training and his readiness to multi-skill he is a long way from making a living from such work:

> I've been trying to find work this whole year in the field, it's always the same sort of answer like we'll hold your résumé and when we get something will call you, sort of thing so. They sometimes ask you for money to lodge your name and résumé.

So Henry is forced to work part time in hospitality, but his job is some distance from where he lives:

> Yeah I do I work in a [five star] hotel … in the city. It's a good job … it's not what I want to do though. So I want to quickly find a job and get out of there. Porter/concierge sort of thing … it's ridiculous. I have a three-hour shift … I have to travel to the city as well so it's like an hour there and just three hours working and an hour back.

Sydney is a sprawling city, in which public transport links are poor, particularly for working-class people living in the outer suburbs. This is one of the bitter ironies of life in global cities: while there are numerous retail, hospitality and service jobs – waiting the tables and cleaning the houses of the professional elite, for example – they are concentrated in places where housing costs prevent those who perform such jobs from living.

Amongst many creative aspirants there is a sense that they are in limbo – waiting for their real lives to begin. This means that they are less likely to start families and commit to long-term relationships than those in other times and places with more secure work. Henry's personal life is on hold while he pursues career ambitions. We asked him if he has a relationship:

> Not at the moment.… I was in one just last year but it was too hard like I just want to concentrate on one thing before I start moving. I don't think there is time because I wouldn't be able to take people out, I've got no time taking out myself now 'cause of all the work and trying to film at the same time.

This is a common predicament of the day-job worker: struggling to keep the creative projects and training alive while making a living in low-paid, precarious work. When asked about what he expects to be doing in five years, his response appears as quixotic yearning rather than practical and realizable:

> Just making a film.… To be known but not known like I want to be known for making films but not like that level of fame where people are sort of talking about me every day or in the newspaper or magazines. I just want to be known I direct movies and that sort of thing, so that's where I would like to be in five years.

However, Henry's dreams appear likely to remain unfulfilled. Although following the conventional advice of risk-taking and creativity, his prospects are hampered by the lack of cultural capital and networks that might open doors. He hints at a dawning realization that class might play a part in limiting his prospects:

> I don't know maybe it's 'cause where we are from or something, the area, I don't know, which just didn't have the same opportunities as others in regards to film.

This is the moment of reckoning. He is a young man and yet he is already referring to his career in the past tense: he *didn't* have the opportunities.

Leonie's life chances

Leonie, in her mid-forties, grew up in the Hunter Valley, to Sydney's north. Her father was a boilermaker and her mother a trained teacher who could only find intermittent work. Leonie had creative ambitions and took a number of short courses in film production and made a couple of films that received some acclaim at local festivals. But she has not really broken through and works in office administration to subsidize her unpaid work on short films. She hunts out networking opportunities and went off to work as a volunteer at the independent Sundance Film Festival, in Canada, but this failed to open doors and she reflects on her stillborn career regretfully and with some self-blame.

Leonie never had the resources to give up her day job and devote herself full-time to film-making and was not prepared to live in abject poverty, influenced by the fear of falling commonly experienced by working-class people (Ehrenreich, 1989):

> I thought that if you are creative, you can't get work; that you have to do something else, you have to have a boring office job to pay the bills.... Maybe I wanted a bit of everything; I wanted my own place, I didn't want to be a starving artist. If, maybe, I was willing to live in a hovel and work crappy jobs at night and not get a lot of sleep, well yeah, [but] I've wanted comfort as well as other things ... it's always been a practicality thing, because I've never wanted to be ridiculously rich but never a starving person living in a house with twenty other people.

We can see how the figure of the artist-bohemian, living hand to mouth, chimes with neo-liberal individualism and its promotion of risk taking and opportunism. Leonie is inclined to take responsibility for her lack of success, despite recognizing the structural obstacles she faces. Walkerdine (2003) characterizes this tendency as 'psychologization', or the interpretation of imposed constraints as personal failings. She believes that she is running out of time, has done very little and has made too many personal sacrifices:

> I don't know, in fact lately I've been having a little 'What will I do with my life?' ... I do go through this every now and then, and I end up in debt and exhausted ... meanwhile I have no personal life, no boyfriend, and I don't have time to do any of that. [But] I am thinking, is this really worth it? And I'm not necessarily getting anywhere ... and sometimes I think I make a lot of excuses, but it's been the practical thing of trying to work other things, unrealistic expectations and even lately I've thought maybe I should give up for a while ... or maybe I haven't tried hard enough.

Leonie's working-class roots are deeply embedded, despite her attempts to escape them. Her parents encouraged her towards office administration/accounts, and what she saw as a day job has now become more long term. Like Henry, in contemplating her fortunes, she reflects on the milieu in which she grew up, her lack of social and cultural capital, and the sort of intrepidness that these things generate:

I think the problem was that I wasn't meeting the right people; everything I did was kind of conservative and so [it was] conservative people that I was meeting. Maybe that's why you don't end up pursuing things, because you are not around people that pursue those things.

Corporate Conscription

Many of our interviewees spoke of pressures from employers to treat their day jobs more seriously, perhaps to identify with its career structures. For most, this would compromise the day-job/creative-career dichotomy that is central to the way they think about their lives. Roger, who subsidized his musical ambitions by working in a hardware store, spoke of liking the job because it did not require him to show any emotional commitment to the corporate mission. He talked of his store work group as if it were a factory-floor community of practice, betraying a slight disdain for managerial direction. When offered the chance to be promoted to managerial level he declined. His creative ambitions represent a rebellion against the sort of white-collar conformity that taking such a role would imply. To be a company man – invested in a corporate career – would be living death. To Roger, the best thing about working on the floor of the hardware shop is the ironic distance from the corporate brand that his co-workers bring to the job: 'Everyone knows it is all bullshit.' And so they build workplace bonds around just getting the job done, and not selling their souls to the company.

Neil, who had dragged his 'sorry arse' back to the pizza shop to reclaim his job after his music dreams came to nothing, recalled that the management had changed and the new proprietors were demanding more than the old.

When I had first worked there the store was operating at a loss and no one really cared, when I went back the management had changed and the manager sat me down … and he said that he had been at Deluxe Pizza for eleven years and takes it very seriously, and I just thought … if I ever, ever turn out like this … please kill me, you know you don't have to take pizza delivery seriously. It is a pizza; you make it, I will take it to someone's house; that is the job … we don't need to have this conversation but you know he was … one of those people who you know worked his way up the Deluxe Pizza ladder, he strongly believed in it and now he has got a lot more stores than he had, and good on him, but you know I just can't … and they use words like family and stuff when they are talking about a job, you know, the 'Deluxe family' … it just makes me want to throw up. I can't stand it.

The Deluxe manager broke the tacit rules of the day-job game: I'll work hard so long as you don't ask me to take it too seriously. In embracing the protest ethos of his music subculture, Neil fiercely resists the corporate earnestness the pizza chain demands of him.

Creative aspirants define the day job as temporary and disposable: something you can leave behind at the end of the working day that should never become the focus of ambition, vocational identification or any other emotional investment. Most importantly, it should never conscript your creative skills. Although those who employ retail and hospitality workers may understand that these people see themselves as lump-labour – low-paid, precarious 'hands' performing tasks under direction – they do not necessarily accept this attitude, as Neil's narrative illustrates. In the new economy, capitalism seeks something more from workers ('Are you passionate about pet accessories?'), sometimes even asking them to hijack their potential for creativity and innovation.

There are some businesses where the bohemian, subcultural and nonconformist tendencies of young workers can complement the corporate brand. Warhurst and Nickson (2007) have argued that service work is no longer uniformly low status, but rather that brand competition in the post-Fordist era has created an occupational hierarchy. Companies – clothing retailers, cafes, bars, restaurants – employ young people with the appropriate 'aesthetic skills', that is, those who embody and express the sort of image the company wishes to communicate. This taps into the youth subcultural registers of cool and breaks with an older ideal of standardized employee servility. Employers encourage customers to identify with their retail employees. Although elite service workers do not have craft skills in the traditional sense, Warhurst and Nickson argue that they are the contemporary aristocrats of labour.

Anne's case illustrates how employers try to 'pick the pockets' of young people to draw on their cultural skills. She was in her mid-teens when she found a part-time job in one of a chain of surf/beachwear shops. A surfer herself, Anne's familiarity with the subculture helped her get the job. The shops are designed in a surf-shack style with lots of timber and a 'graffiti' aesthetic, selling T-shirts with bright cartoon designs, irreverent slogans and snippets of wry, homespun philosophy. The shirts are marketed mainly to young men, while young women customers mostly buy skirts, dresses and swimwear. In keeping with the hip, thin beach look, the shop only carries small and medium sizes. Workers are expected to buy and wear the shop merchandise, and are given a clothing allowance. They are trained to adopt an informal approach to customers in keeping with the brand's youth-friendly image. Far from requiring a 'customer is always right' deference, Anne's employers expected her to be chatty and relaxed when trying to sell clothes, and to use interactions with customers as an opportunity to do some surreptitious research:

> [My employers were] really up on the 'just relax' and really easy going, don't worry about things. They used to make us write on the sheet why they were buying the garment. We used to have to talk to the customers and find things out about them … to be their friend … be easy going and help out a bit … laid back and cool.

In encouraging her to approach customers as peers, Anne's employers sought to conceal service/sales relationships – to reconceive it as a meeting of peers (Zwick and Kayla, 2011, pp. 220–2). Yet their expectation that sales staff identify with corporate goals demonstrates the phoniness of this youthful bonding. This typifies what Hochschild (2003) terms 'emotional labour': employers' demands that workers contrive affect/feelings – smiling, expressing warmth and familiarity – beyond what should be reasonably expected when dealing with customers in a service occupation. Anne recalled that there were tensions with her manager over the demand that she compete to meet sales targets: '[W]e could just shrug off when we didn't make the target sales. It just wasn't as important to us.' The workers' subcultural capital (Thornton, 1995), which was so valuable to the brand image, could not be reconciled with the corporate enthusiasm that employers expected workers to display. The surfies' nonconformism, their rejection of ambition and materialism, was incompatible with the drive to maximize sales.

This illustrates a wider trend where retail and hospitality employers seek to recruit those whose appearance/presentation/attitude chimes with the image they seek to communicate. Pettinger, who conducted an ethnography of service work in fashionable clothing shops, found that those who worked there were an essential part of the brand marketing:

> There are significant tangible and intangible elements of the retail experience […] including the nature of the service culture and the extension of the branded design environment to incorporate the sales assistants themselves. (Pettinger, 2004, p. 180)

Aesthetic skills can range from the subcultural to the highbrow, as the example of Niamh illustrates. While living in the UK in gap year before starting a degree in media studies/journalism, she worked in London's Covent Garden as a sales assistant for one of a chain of stores selling expensive clothing and accessories. (*It was conservative but trendy and elegant kind of styling*

of clothes. A lot of silk, a lot of hand beaded, a lot of fine-cut linens.) As part of
the interview process for the job, Niamh was required to approach a staff
member posing as a customer and suggest items of clothing that would suit
her. In this 'audition' process, her prospective employers were assessing her
aesthetic skills:

> They were looking for people who could mix and match things. They
> didn't want someone working there who had no colour-scheme sense.
> I guess you had to have a certain amount of fashion sense.

Niamh was asked to wear the company merchandise – sold to her on a staff
discount – as many clothing retail workers are, both at work (as required) and
elsewhere. The corporate harnessing of creative skills is not limited to the
forms of appearance and presentation, but also includes spoken communication. Call centres employ out-of-work actors (Brophy, 2011), who they believe
have the requisite skills for cold-calling, telephone sales and market research.
Hochschild (2003) argues that this is a modern form of alienation, but that it
is alienation nevertheless. While it appears less degrading than monotonous
factory work, in many ways it resembles the alienated labour of those who
operate machines on a production line.

Conclusion

The mythology of the artist is of a person completely immersed in their art,
and not distracted by workaday concerns (Simpson, 1981). But artists and
aspiring creative workers living in expensive cities often have to find a day job
to survive. The idea of the day job is as much a cultural construction as an
economic arrangement. It is a semantic device to organize the inner narrative
of working life. *I'm doing this to pay the bills while waiting for my career to take off.* It is
what you go to, or go back to, if plans for your 'real life' have stalled or have
yet to be realized. In times and places where career jobs (whether creative or
otherwise) – full time, secure and well-paid – are relatively abundant, then
workers can have confidence that they will eventually be able to make the
transition from low-paid, irregular and insecure work. Similarly, those with the
cultural, social and economic capital can have some confidence that they will
eventually get a career break, and so they are more able to cheerfully toler-
ate the day job, making a virtue made of necessity. But with the general rise
of precarious work, and the decline of professional opportunities, such jobs
form a sort of vortex from which many find it difficult to escape. Employers
can benefit from the day-job mentality: those who see their jobs as temporary
are less likely to make industrial demands for better wages, conditions and

job security. However, this does not mean that employers are willing to accept workers' diffidence and dissociation from corporate goals. When it comes to performance targets, they demand a modern sensibility rather than postmodern detachment. Indeed, in the context of competitive and differentiated markets in retail and hospitality, many seek to use both subtle and direct means to conscript workers' emotional investments and creative/aesthetic skills. This, of course, is resisted because subculture and bohemianism rebels against capitalism, and forms its counterpoint and conscience.

Chapter 5

LABILE LABOUR

Policies promoting labour flexibility erode processes of relational and peer-group interaction that are vital for reproducing skills and constructive attitudes to work. If you expect to change what you are doing at almost any time, to change 'employer' at short notice, to change colleagues and above all to change what you call yourself, work ethics become constantly contestable and opportunistic.

Guy Standing *The Precariat*

At this point, it is worth recapping the argument with which we opened this book. Economic change in the West has made the directions of working life more difficult to fathom. Jobs and careers that once appeared stable seem more and more precarious, as do skills, both those acquired on the job and through education. In societies where communal and social supports have eroded, people are increasingly made responsible for their own fate. Policymakers and educators have encouraged workers to develop their creative skills, arguing that the West's future prosperity depends on symbolic and intellectual innovation. Such an injunction strikes a popular chord at two levels. Firstly, it accords with a radical critique of soul-destroying, Taylorised work that has its roots in both the 1960s counterculture (a largely middle-class movement) and in working-class resistance to alienated labour. The creativity injunction appears to offer an alternative to moral conformity, mass production and consumption and the conventional scripts of working life. It finds expression in popular culture, particularly televised talent shows (now a subgenre of 'reality television'), where contestants can find fame in a variety of creative endeavours – singing, dancing, cooking, modelling. Secondly, the creativity injunction appeals to youth, particularly those who resist or don't fit in at school. Such people can easily become lost in the fog in the journey to adulthood and the idea of a creative career suggests the possibility of bridging subculture/youth culture and adult life. Where once such cultures seemed hermetically sealed against the workaday world – forming a parallel universe where only imaginary solutions to alienated adult life were possible – now youthful symbolic play receives pedagogical and technocratic encouragement. Most of our interviewees related their vocational aspirations to those freewheeling youth cultural practices. In the creative economy even resistant subculture can provide a foundation for life. Boltanski and Chiapello (2006) argue that these forms of accommodation represent capitalism's versatility, and in particular its ability to regenerate, modernize and humanize in the face of critique, absorbing certain demands while deflecting others that might undermine the bedrock of social and economic power.

In flying the flag of creativity, new capitalism has succeeded in stretching the term to connote not just aesthetic innovation but certain dispositions of labour: individualism, opportunism and promiscuous aspiration – a readiness to transfer skills and enthusiasms towards the opportunities the market throws up. There are contradictions at the heart of this project to remake labour, however, that contradict the sanguine, even utopian, visions for working life held by those who advocate this new creative flexibility. In the face of insufficient and insecure work, the creative career must be improvised. Aspirants must live with churn, with erratic work patterns, and embrace these conditions of uncertainty. They must be prepared to take on day jobs to finance their larger aspirations, and commit their social lives to building the contacts on which work opportunities depend. This is not just about meeting the right people. It is also about presenting yourself in a way that will mark you as worthy and cool.

Adversity can lead to the deflection and qualification of creative ambition. In the oversupplied labour markets, aspirants soon learn that they exercise less sovereignty over their fate than neo-liberalism might suggest. Consequently, they are limited to exercising what we term *improvisational agency*.[1] At the point where they are met with poverty, lack of opportunity and a shrinking range of options, they are forced to recalibrate their ambitions and transfer their skills. How do they respond to the rigours of the gig economy? Can they emulate the model of the flexible, individualist worker? Can they maintain the imaginary bridge from the ludic to the vocational, which appears so central to creative identity, in situations where aspirations are bartered and dissimulated? In these circumstances, how are identities reworked and biographical narratives recomposed?

In order to understand the 'creative career', the fortunes of those who embark on this career and their ability to endure its vicissitudes, it is necessary to go beyond the conventional frame for understanding creative work and to

---

1 Similar to what Evans (2007) refers to as bounded agency.

consider a broader range of influences on occupational socialization. To survive in turbulent labour markets, most creative aspirants must become what we term *labile labour*: mobile, spontaneous, malleable and capable of being aroused by new vocational possibilities. They must also present as eager and ambitious, but, paradoxically, this ambition must be diffuse. These dispositions can be contrasted with those of Taylorist labour: stable, dependable and inert, the factory hands amenable to managerial direction. Specifically, the qualities required of the new worker include, firstly, an ability to view skills as abstract and transferable, rather than as grounded, singular and non-negotiable. Under the conditions of new capitalism, of rapid technological and stylistic change and innovation, the permutations of working life are less foreseeable. As Rose argues, contemporary workers should 'engage in skilling, reskilling, enhancement of credentials and preparation for a life of incessant job seeking: Life is to become a continuous economic capitalization of the self' (Rose, 1999, p. 161). Secondly, the labile worker must bring individualistic and competitive inclinations to working life, a readiness to improvise and 'rebrand' in response to this change and innovation. In Adkins's and Lury's terms, the new worker is involved in an ongoing project of reflexivity:

> A self-transforming subject – who can constantly adapt his or her performance of a self-identity and who can claim the effects of that performance of self-identity to define their own goals (to fill in the blanks along the way) – is figured as the ideal subject of the employment contract. (1999: 601)

Thirdly, the new worker must be capable of recognizing and being excited by serendipitous opportunities, wherever and whenever they arise, through friendship, family and community networks as well as vocational contacts (Gill, 2010; Taylor and Littleton, 2012). Fourthly, the new worker must be prepared to endure the scrutiny and arbitrary judgements of gatekeepers in those occupations where work is usually allocated informally. To challenge the legitimacy, credentials and caprice of those exercising this judgement is to mark oneself as unworthy. In the following pages we will argue that men from working-class and minority backgrounds, in particular, find it difficult to perform the role of labile labour.

Gender and the Gig Economy

Several writers (Adkins, 2000; Gill, 2002, 2009; Banks & Milestone, 2011) have suggested that the the gig economy throws up tripwires for women, even that it *re-traditionalizes* gender roles (Adkins, 1999, 2000). For women who are primary carers or who shoulder an unequal burden of domestic labour, the uncertain rhythms of precarious work – subcontracting, 'permalancing' and casual employment – are far from ideal. Those caring responsibilities can prevent women from earning a regular and sufficient income, and it can prevent them from engaging in the sorts of networking activities through which informal recruitment takes place. While working for large employers, by contrast, women generally can see more stable career structures and enjoy more protection from discrimination through discrimination/complaints-resolution processes.

While these arguments are certainly valid, it is also important to recognize that the values and habits associated with what we might call Fordist masculinity can work against creative flexibility. While blue-collar work is rapidly declining, the habits associated with that work – what Cohen (1999) terms the cultural codes of working-class masculinity – endure. They are embodied in various practices and values, for example, in the informal and mimetic ways in which men learn new skills, and in the general hostility to the scrutiny and evaluation of those external to workplace communities of practice (echoing the resistance to professional and bureaucratic oversight of manual work). Such cultures can be recovered in places other than the factory floors: both in places of formal learning – workshops and studios, in schools, colleges and universities, where artistic, musical, media, design skills are taught – and informal learning – in garages, backyards, gyms and on sporting fields. Masculine codes are recovered in such spaces even where the social and economic arrangements that produced them are in decline.

Cohen (1999) contrasts the code of apprenticeship with that of career, and identifies the former with old masculinity. The apprenticeship system had historical roots in the pre-modern guild and trade system, but was central to Fordist production. Skilled trades/craft work involved the use of 'implements of labour [that] were often thought of as a kind of prosthetic extension of bodily skill, moulded by customary usages of handicraft' (1999, p. 132). Tradesmen and craftsmen, the aristocrats of labour, were a breed apart from unskilled labourers and exercised what Cohen calls a 'specialised dexterity' (1999, p. 132) in working raw materials with tools. Importantly, access to this 'patrimony of skill [...] always entailed an apprenticeship'. This involved becoming submerged in communities of practice – many of which were based on communal and familial recruitment – in which learning occurred through observation and emulation (Lave and Wenger, 1991; Wenger, 1998). This is not simply a narrative of skill, but also one of the social relations in which those skills are developed. Hollands refers to this as 'cultural apprenticeship' and describes how this helped to develop 'a peculiarly masculine shop-floor culture' (1990, p. 103). The meritocratic code of career, by contrast with apprenticeship, values external credentials over on-the-job, mimetic training.

Researchers (Kenway et al., 2006; McDowell, 2000; Nixon, 2006) have already demonstrated that there are obstacles faced by men in performing affective or emotional labour – dealing with customers/clients and other tasks associated with the service and caring professions. But in this chapter we will show that the cultural codes shape vocational identities in ways that may not be compatible with the demands of creative work.

Designer Douglas

Douglas was a rebellious youth and failed to complete high school. Lucky to get a trade apprenticeship as a sheet-metal worker, he spent four years exposed to factory-floor culture. He 'hated every minute of it' but was driven by his mother to complete the apprenticeship, despite knowing that this was not what he 'wanted to do in life'. With hindsight, he makes a virtue out of perseverance. Later, as a student in a design course at technical college, he spoke of the value of the skills he obtained during his apprenticeship.

> Looking back on it now I learnt a lot of skills … I can make stuff and it is awesome. I didn't like it because of the [factory] environment, I like making stuff, I still tinker and kind of like just doing stuff around the house and making things, like I make jewellery at home just on the side and sell that, and it helps me heaps here, like I am ten steps ahead of everyone else because I have the knowledge of making stuff.

Douglas has laboured to transpose his skills, from an industrial to a post-industrial setting. He retains a sense of craftsmanship, however. The economic or industry imperative, in other words, has not yet taken over. Consequently, he struggles to reconcile the sort of self-reconstruction required if he is to become a successful designer, a highly competitive and precarious field.

Douglas's design education covers not just skills training, but provides a broader cultural initiation to the field and the social and cultural skills that are required to succeed in it. Like many of our interviewees, he spoke of being given a primer in the importance of getting to know and becoming memorable to cultural brokers – studio and gallery operators, agents, dealers and retailers. He quickly became aware of the hierarchical character of design, where very few become auteurs and most remain on the exploited edges of the industry. The Design Industry of Australia figures suggest that there are nearly seven thousand fashion, industrial and jewellery designers, the same number of interior designers and thirty-five thousand graphic and web designers and illustrators (Lacey, 2013). This vastly oversupplies the market and only counts those who identify. The organization's president, Oliver Kratzer, stated:

> Everybody loves to study design and all the universities supply a multitude of design degree courses but with little correlation to actual demand. (Lacey, 2013)

Douglas is forced to reckon with the injunction to market himself, to network, to develop a personal brand or style. These things don't come naturally to him because he has a tendency to pour scorn on pompous, phony and self-aggrandizing forms of behaviour. His straightforward, down-to-earth disposition is at odds with the design world, which requires an ability to dissimulate.

> They are wanker designers and I didn't know this at the start, but yeah I don't reckon I could act like they are, not most of them. Just the ones that you see in the media you know what I mean. … But I have already decided that I am not going to lose my integrity if I do make it because … you know what I am talking about, black turtle-necks and the glasses?

Here Douglas refers to a vocation expectation that he is still seeking to fathom, in which branding and performance (and aesthetic skills, see Warhurst and Nickson, 2007) are more important than the skills you possess, the quality of your work. For those, like Douglas, who arrive in the hyper-real, entrepreneurial field of design, and who have very little experience of creative work, and few family and community narratives to draw on, or advice to guide them, the realization that they will be judged on how hip they are, rather than how good their work is, is bewildering and salutary. He feels that to respond to these pressures towards dissimulation would mean that he would lose his integrity. The idea of the authentic masculine self that refuses to perform to the crowd, to strangers and outsiders, runs very deep for Douglas and for many others whom we interviewed (see Bourgois, 1995). We can see how his years as an apprentice led him to embrace a no-nonsense working-class persona, something that is functional to the factory floor, but which is anathema to the world of the new economy:

> Nothing wrong with blue collar work at all like a lot of my mates are tradesmen but I just want something more I guess, and something into design, like I fell into design.

Here Douglas describes the biographical project of straddling the old and the new economy. Sheet-metal work represents old labour, manual trade skills central to industrial workplaces, but with the decline in demand for those skills, as metal-processing work goes offshore, he seeks to recalibrate. This appears in the narrative as being the product of choice ('I just want something more') but is also strategic, part of a larger biographical project to avoid redundancy as old work gives way to new.

Maker Mahmoud

Mahmoud's father worked in various trades before establishing a small business, a common strategy taken by immigrant workers in Australia seeking independence from wage labour. He had grown up in war-torn Lebanon, living in a village close to the Israeli border, before migrating and working in various trades but, like many migrants, had his ambitions curtailed:

> He is a mechanic, a plumber, carpenter, electrician, plumber, you name it, he would have loved to do something in aviation but couldn't.

His business involved installing kitchens. When Mahmoud finished school his father asked him to join him in the business but Mahmoud refused:

> I told him no, and I wanted to get another job, we had a massive fight over it and the whole family got involved, which wasn't good.

Mahmoud resisted the scripted prospect of working in the building trades – like many in his family and community – in the quest for something more creatively fulfilling. At school he had been inspired by his art teacher – 'She gave us the right to be whatever we liked … and art was sort of like a freedom and escape.' – to the point where, in the mid-teenage years, he preferred being in the art room to being at home: 'When I was on holidays I used to go to school and do my artwork there, instead of going home and make a mess [and Mum] … telling me off.'

Mahmoud's school grades were not good enough to get him into university. He wanted to continue studying art, but needed a course that would mollify his parents' concerns about his employability. So he applied for a place in a graphic design course at a technical college, expressing a sentiment commonly heard amongst young people striving to resist lives of repetitive manual work: 'Like you have got that chance to express yourself more passionately.' However, like many people from poor backgrounds, he was walking blindly into a creative field with few work or career prospects:

> I got knocked back because I didn't really know what it was, and like I thought it was just an extension of art except you go more into the business side of things.

He enrolled instead in a digital media course with the intention of transferring to graphic design after one year and told us that he would apply to study at university if his grades were sufficient.

Like others, Mahmoud tried to parlay a cultural enthusiasm into a vocationally viable credential prompted by the encouragement he received for his creative talents. But with little knowledge of job prospects, nor contacts to help him succeed in oversupplied labour markets, he would struggle to survive. Additionally, we get the sense that there are aspects of residual masculinity that work against the niceties expected from a freelancing creative worker. Mahmoud tells the story of conflict that his father had with a customer that he observed when he was helping with the installation of a kitchen:

> We were putting the kickboard … and she saw a speck of dust underneath there, she was like, 'what are you doing you are ruining my floor', and … she started complaining and whinging and my dad turned to her, 'Listen if you don't like it that is it I will leave the stuff here, I will pack up my tools and I will go see you later.' She accepted it.

Mahmoud reflected on how he would handle these sorts of demands in working to commission briefs for graphic design. The thing that drew him, and most others, to art/symbolic work in the first place was the ludic autonomy, the magical insulation of the creative space and the support of the artistic community of practice. But to succeed as a commissioned designer he would have to compromise his independence and meet client expectations. Traditional workers resisted interference from those whose understanding of what they do was, at best, only abstract and theoretical, and at worst, nonexistent. While the artist is very different from the trade/manual worker, there is something in Mahmoud's description of his early experiences of dealing with commissioned work that suggests that he is brittle, reluctant to assimilate to the demands of the freelancing life:

> At the moment I am doing a job for myself with a client and she sees all these great things and all this other stuff, I am more than happy to do it for her because I love doing what I love doing … [but] the way I see it, like if you get knocked back by people it is just I take it as … 'If they don't want the type of stuff that I like to do then they can go and find someone else that they like.'

Take it or leave it. This is my work. I will not dance to your tune. This represents both the tension between the personas of artist and creative worker – the difficulty of making that transition from the independent, 'passionate' artist to the flexible gun-for-hire and the worker's resistance to outside interference.

The other frame for understanding this narrative is around the idea of service work, the sovereign customer and emotional labour. Nixon (2009) noted that the notion that the 'customer is always right' grates with the model of the taciturn, brittle and implacable working-class masculinity. We are suggesting here that there are residual working-class masculine sensibilities that structure the way kids like Mahmoud inhabit the identity of artist in the first place and that limit their capacity to reinvent themselves as creative freelancers.

Tony's artisanal calling

We discussed Tony in Chapter 2: the son of working-class Italian immigrants who worked as commercial cleaners and discouraged his ambition to become a film editor. ('Is this job going to pay the bills? Is it going to give you a pay packet?') Despite this, he devotes much of his young adult life to training courses which have yielded very little paid work. He spoke about learning from the seasoned professionals who taught him (and who are unable to make a living themselves from editing) in terms of a craft apprenticeship and the importance of conserving artisanal skills in the face of technology:

> I guess in as far as finding a mentor, one of our editing teachers, he'll come into our suites individually and … I think we admire him a lot because he's more old school, doing it for years, respected in the industry, you know, editors that are competent enough to use the computer they edit on but that's not where they learnt their craft from. … People are under the impression that to be an editor, it's about learning to use the software very well but they don't really know much about the craft of editing [and] maybe it's not necessarily their own fault because you have to go to a school that have teachers that are working editors or retired editors who can teach the old, traditional way, and it's more about technology now.

New technologies guarantee standardization but remove judgement, craft skill, and the imperfections that can make cultural products quirky and interesting. Similar attitudes were apparent among the largely male music-production students we interviewed. Although they were impressed with the state-of-the-art equipment available to them at their technical college, they also had a deep respect for those raised on 'old-school' techniques. Tony also embraces the idea that the work should combine both craft and artistic skills:

> [You can learn] on the job but the sorts of things you can't learn has to come from yourself, having that emotion and intuition of telling stories and that came natural to me. That's what it's really about … you do it on a subconscious level.

His aspirations reflect the reaction to Taylorism, the critique of alienated work, by recuperating the aesthetic dimension, but also a desire to conserve the artisanal element of slow accretion of craft skills learned through observation and trial-and-error, hands-on practice.

But his training has produced few opportunities. He volunteered in a production house but this experience left him intensely disillusioned:

> I was just doing bits and pieces of stuff that other people weren't doing. And pretty much the owner, I worked as his camera assistant, you know did some other things here and there, learnt a couple of things but then I thought, how much more can you learn when all you do is the same thing over again? How do you exactly make the move from working in these small production houses doing corporate stuff... you're the guy who dabbles in everything – I'm the editor, I'm the photoshop guy, I'm the after-effects guy, the colourist, sound designer whatever else. Make lunch, bring coffee – well everyone's gotta do that in the beginning ... [but] all they seem to do is focus on cranking out cheap, corporate stuff? That's boring, banal and then you may learn to be more of a technical person but creatively you're doomed, you just die in there.

Tony is far from being the flexible subject of the creative industries. His investment in the craft-artist identity is deep rooted and indivisible. Not willing to 'rebrand' or transfer skills superficially, nor improvise for the sake it, he would prefer to salvage whatever creative integrity he can by avoiding the fate of 'cranking out cheap corporate stuff'. He accepts the short-term need to multiskill and to work around corporate imperatives but only as a means to achieving some greater creative autonomy later on. This would appear to be a vain hope.

Jake and the lost community of practice

By contrast with Tony, Jake has been successful in finding craft work in the film industry, in a specialized niche: designing and producing animatronic puppets for fantasy, science fiction and children's films.[2] Growing up in a small rural town, but with a strong artistic/countercultural community, Jake played in a successful band as a teenager, and spent some time on a school work-experience programme with a man who made latex puppets for the film

---

2 Banks (2010) has argued that craft labour has been under-represented in the literature on creative work, as researchers focus on artistic labour instead.

industry. This sparked his interest because the craft, specialized, project-based work seemed to combine new and old skills: employing the same technology as mechanized cars that he played with as a child, and the design skills that he learned in a well-resourced school workshop. Jake had fond memories of his teachers and especially those who taught him in informal settings, in his music and design/technology classes. It became clear that it was not only the pleasure at both mechanical and aesthetic free play that he experienced in these settings but also the cultures of informal learning and the communities of practice that he found in the classroom. Additionally, Jake spoke of spending time with his father, a bus driver, fixing cars and motorbikes, doing mechanical things in the garage.

Later on, while living and working in a mundane job in Sydney, he got a break when he learned 'that the creature department on [a feature film project] needed a runner'. So he called and got the job. This allowed him to hang around the edges of the work group of model makers and eventually to be accepted and learn their techniques. Eventually he was able to set up his own business but the work has always been project based, highly specialized and intermittent. As a freelancer in the early stages of his career, he makes a reasonable living (unlike most of our interviewees) from his puppet-making work but nevertheless voiced regret at the individualistic and competitive structures that the film industry imposes on his trade. We asked him about his attitude to his peers:

> I wouldn't want to be competition, I just want to work with them, for them … I've put so many hours into people's stuff before and get no gratitude and I watch them do it to other people … yeah, there's a lot of people that do that, take that angle but then they're constantly trying to get stuff out of you and you help them, like I still will help them. I don't know why I do but I do.

He gives freely but often without reciprocation ('Like I still will help them. I don't know why but I do.') but is frustrated with those whose selfish guarding of knowledge disrupt the community of practice:

> Yeah, I'm lucky I've had a lot of help from so many different people, that's the most important thing, and I help those people out heaps, like the guys I work for, I help them with stuff where most people would charge them. They give me materials sometimes and I help them do other things … [and] I appreciate it when people help me and a lot people I work with don't, and they're the sort of people I have zero time for, that's just pathetic.

This illustrates the residual influence of the culture of craft collaboration. Jake has successfully made the transition from old to new labour, has added specialized aesthetic skills to both mechanical and digital knowledge. He has found craft-artist work in the film industry (Banks, 2010), but is unhappy about the individualist structures of the relations of production. By relating nostalgic narratives about the informal teaching and learning of his youth, he shows a yearning for the relations of mutual support in which trade skills were traditionally practised.

Matt's craft values

We briefly introduced Matt in Chapter 2. The son of a bus-driver single father whose mother died young, and who enrolled in a music production course at a technical college after completing school. He also played bass in a band and harboured ambitions to make a living from playing music. Matt told us that he had always chosen to study what excited him, rather than being concerned about career and financial security. Despite bringing up four children on very little money, Matt's father encouraged his creative ambition, and Matt appeared relatively calm and optimistic about the future despite understanding the risks involved.

He approached the study of music production as if it were a trade apprenticeship. This involved looking upon music as a craft, and treating the teachers as crafts mentors. He appreciated the hands-on pedagogy, talked of the importance of 'old-school' analogue technologies and was worried about the potential corruption of musicianship by digital technology and commercialization:

> You may get this fantastic little band will come [into the] studio, you'll think God these guys are brilliant … but they won't have much backing behind them. So you've got to do it short, quickly and on a tight schedule. You've got to come to a point where you can say no, we've got to stop, we've got to move on to something else guys and they may not be 100 per cent happy with what they've got and you could sit there thinking if we just track this band one more time and said everyone just do one more take, you could get the best take ever. It would be absolutely perfect but you can't do that. Or you get someone who's been picked up by a major label but has … no talent … and they're spending … thousands of dollars to use your recording studio and just have unlimited time and funds to go and produce this album which they're never going to play perfectly on or sing perfectly on or whatever. But there's electronic mediums available to help you correct that.

He talks about refusing to participate in using production techniques to paper over the shortcomings of musicians – digitally enhancing the sound of those with poor skills:

> Our studio teacher, he teaches everything about the recording studio. He showed us little bits and pieces that people use to cheat and do all this other stuff but he doesn't teach to use it like that. He teaches us to use it as an aid, he teaches us to really think about what we're doing and get it right on our own accord not sit there in post-production and just completely rip something apart and stick it back together.

He went to see a local band after hearing their music on social media only to find that they could not match the recording when performing live: 'They got up on stage and it was absolutely horrible.' These narratives reflect his commitment to what he sees as traditional craft values – to not crossing the line between being a producer and effectively 'ghostwriting' the music.

The pressures to make a living make this a difficult ethical line to walk, and Matt tells us that studying gave him a realistic picture of job prospects in the industry. As a young man he had naively optimistic rock-music dreams – 'oh yeah, find a booking agent, gets signed, we'll be huge' – but was quickly disabused of this youthful arrogance after starting the production course at college. He became aware of the need to multiskill and of the amount of work required for even modest success:

> The industry is about working hard and being able to adapt. I'd love to be going out and playing every night and making huge amounts of money off it but I doubt that's going to happen. … So I'm content to go out and break even. As it is we perform at a loss basically, it costs us money to get there and petrol, eating … by the time you get there and you get home again it's cost you about 40 to 50 bucks. That's fine, I make up my losses by working as a sound technician when and where I can. … The term jack of all trades and master of none is perfectly applicable to the industry … you could be hugely skilled in one facet of it but that won't guarantee you a meal on the table the next day.

While studying, Matt was able to obtain some work in producing bands at small pub venues in Sydney and discusses the satisfaction he derives from being part of a team:

> In a band it's a team, you're all working towards one goal but you will contribute on different levels in different ways. The same with technical

production, you're part of a team. … It doesn't matter if you plug in an XRR lead into the stage box on a multi-core or if you are actually the front-of-house operator, you're part of a team and you do a job. If you do it well and you do it with pride there is so much satisfaction to be had from it. It is a very thankless job and being a sound technician because you're not like the musos, you're not up on stage, not everyone sees you … you will get a couple of musicians every now and then who will come up to you and say, 'mate, that was brilliant thank you so much', they'll shake your hand, they might even buy you a beer. That's what makes it worth it, just knowing – or even if they're up on stage and they say 'thanks to the production crew', it's to every one of the production crew not just you, everyone. I think the team environment is what I enjoy best about it.

Like other young men we interviewed, Matt appears to yearn for the sort of solidarity akin to blue-collar communities of practice, where the bonds between workers count for more than the critical assessment of outsiders. The music industry provides fleeting neo-tribal possibilities to experience such social bonds, but those working in it are among the most precarious and vulnerable of creative workers. They must constantly work to reproduce their professional identities, to keep the work coming in. If Matt cannot make a living from music, he will move in a completely new vocational direction. He does not see his music skills as abstract and transferable to jobs outside the industry. Rather, his fallback is to become a motorcycle mechanic, because of his longstanding interest in bikes:

I think my most – my secondary career if you will, my backup career would probably be a motorcycle mechanic … it's something you do. You can take pride in your work … you've gone through this engine and you've pulled it apart piece by piece and put it back together.

His principal concern is that such a job would deprive him of the camaraderie he experiences while making and producing music.

Hayley and the main chance

Hayley grew up poor in the western suburbs of Sydney:

… always had hand-me-downs, bikes and clothes … never had lunch money, got a [school] lunch order on my birthday, still take a packed lunch everywhere and I think hard before buying something and I'd get pocket money and save it.

When she left school she worked in shops and offices. Hayley spoke of not feeling family pressure in relation to her work choices. Rather, she was encouraged to find her calling: 'I've always gone with the flow and mum's always just been, "do whatever you like, whatever makes you happy, it'll work out."' She exemplifies the qualities of the new worker: eagerness but with tractable ambition and a singular and all-consuming commitment to work (Gregg, 2011):

> What I put my mind to I do well because I'm really determined … whatever I apply myself to and as long as you set your mind to it, it will happen and there's an addiction to success. … It's just I've never really known what I wanted to do, still don't know, even now, so totally fell into it. … But for me to get that far I've had to push really hard and for me to go further I need to push harder… your life becomes your work and you can't do this career without it taking over your life.

She sees her skills as transferable, and her career is structured according to industry rather than craft imperatives. Being 'determined' suggests a willingness to improvise, to reshape her ambitions and occupational identity in pursuit of 'success', and importantly, to build her networks, which are looser forms of association than communities of practice. Her media career began in the creative arts and communications course through which she found her way into broadcast television. As one of a group of student interns at 'GMT' television, she saw it as necessary to stand out from the crowd, to be noticed, rather than treating her peers as a community of practice:

> I remember when I walked through the doors at GMT I was like, I am not leaving here. … I would always keep away from all the other students because I just wanted to be on my own so the people there, it wasn't the group from uni it was always just Hayley they were talking to and stuff … and just because I'm a bit chatty and friendly with people and I'll often talk my ideas through with people there. … [And] I'm good at calling people and getting through to the right people.

Hayley was recognized by those with the power to offer work opportunities, where the others were not, although these were always short term and part time. However, she seeks to make a virtue out of her precarious circumstances, internalizing the creative-economy discourse that sees vocational restlessness as guaranteeing renewal. Like many of the young women we interviewed, but rarely the men, Hayley embraces a sense of fatalism about the direction of her working life, resisting the temptation to try to engineer outcomes:

> I think in terms of one year, I just don't really think further than that so I'm trying to relax and not be such a controlling person, tell myself that everything falls into place.

Hayley is happy to surrender to the judgement of the creative gatekeepers, and the fatalism allows her to steel herself against the inevitable rejections that are part of the creative career. Under the code of apprenticeship, by contrast, the community of practice is the primary source for legitimating skill and conferring vocational esteem, and the arbitrary judgement of outsiders is regarded with contempt. As we saw in Chapter 3, Nada described the experience of being 'discovered' and being offered a job in the music industry, after a chance encounter with a customer while she was working in a clothing store in an upmarket part of Sydney. 'This was my chance to shine', she said, in terms reminiscent of the language of those who audition their creative talents – from cooking, to designing, modelling and various performing arts – on reality-television programmes.

Theresa's magical realism

Theresa, around thirty, grew up in a northern New South Wales town 'on an old hippy commune really' and her class background is difficult to specify. Like several others in our sample, she had an artist-bohemian father who subsidized his unpaid creative endeavours with low-wage labour and the family was relatively poor. She moved to the city to take a sound engineering course but didn't enjoy the technical demands, dropped out and, at the suggestion of her sister, turned her interests to film. Her break came after she overheard a conversation between fellow customers in café, one of whom was lamenting their inability to find a styling assistant for a film shoot:

> I heard this girl beside me going oh my god, I've got this shoot and I need a styling assistant and I can't find one anywhere, and I looked over [and said] excuse me, I just heard you mention that and I'm a styling assistant so I got a contact and straight on the job.

Not particularly bound to a fixed creative vocation, Theresa is able to recognize and take advantage of diverse opportunities and the serendipitous moments that often define the creative career narrative. Later she became a location scout. Working for low pay for a film-production company she saw the opportunity to move sideways:

I was actually out scouting one day and I was knocking on a door to look for some house for a commercial and this lady answered and I said hi I'm a location scout … and she said oh my god I've just moved here from England and I've started up my own location company and you know, I'm looking for someone … she said what do you charge, I knew the other scouts at the other place were getting like $300 a day so I told her $300 a day, I can't believe the words came out of my mouth, like I got this air of confidence about myself and she said … I'd love to have you come work for me.

She speaks of her life as littered with incidents of happenstance and, like Hayley, rationalizes this in the language of fatalism and teleology: nothing has meaning until the final unravelling is clear and what happens is 'meant to be'. Such a Zen-like disposition allows her to weather the vagaries of the creative career, and to break with the idea of a fixed idea of creative skill or talent:

I think I'm just a big believer in the way that energy works; you put energy out there and it comes back, like there's no way that it doesn't. I just don't believe that if you're out there doing things whether you're getting paid or not, if you're just out there doing things, things will happen, they just have to. I've always just believed that.

Like Hayley, Theresa is a much more supple vocational subject than the young men we discuss above, one who is able to reshape herself in response to the random interpellations of the volatile creative-labour markets. It is this more diffuse notion of art and calling that equips her to become a 'slashie' (stylist – slash – location scout and so forth: a multiskilled young adult).

Amanda's diffuse ambitions

We discussed Amanda in Chapter 2: the daughter of a single mother, who grew up in Newcastle, New South Wales, living in squats in 'bohemian poverty'. She described the memory of a primary-school teacher praising her creative writing as having kindled her creative aspirations. She also spoke about them almost as a genetic inevitability, drawing on what Cohen calls the *narrative code of inheritance* (Cohen, 1999):

Well, I had no choice really, I think I was destined to have a creative career. My parents were both creative; my mother is a visual artist and my father [who died when she was young] a musician, so that was a highly prized ability in my home.

Amanda studied film-making at university, but, with very little experience apart from volunteering on student productions, she found it difficult to get a job after graduating. She tried conventional job-seeking methods:

> [After uni I] checked the paper, sent out 100 CVs to 100 production companies in Sydney. I didn't question it, I just thought that [was] normal, I thought that's what you did and I got three interviews … and yeah, [there were] no jobs out there.

Despite taking all the right steps – checking job advertisements, writing formal applications, cold-calling potential employers – nothing eventuated. As we have seen, few film industry jobs are advertised; most are allocated via word of mouth through existing networks. ('And I was really quite shocked when I realized that [my degree] was essentially a worthless piece of tertiary paper.') This experience was salutary and presented Amanda with the sort of dilemma faced by others we have looked at in this book: how to stay afloat when work is scarce. Fortunately, her vocational identity was not governed by either craft independence or artistic romanticism. So unlike others, she was willing to see her film-making skills as transferable and to apply them in unanticipated ways. She quickly realized that there was little money to support emerging film directors and started a business producing educational videos for clients in the public and private sector.

> I didn't get into any of this expecting to be freelance, but I had no alternative. … So I became freelance almost by accident. … My grandfather was [a small entrepreneur] … so maybe I take more after him.

Eventually she began teaching others how to be freelancers, running courses in business and entrepreneurship skills at various education institutions from community colleges to universities. ('I have a compulsion to teach, so whenever I learn something new, I want to teach it to someone else.') Part of her pedagogical approach was to talk about her early life, highlighting the nonconventional and countercultural aspects of it, to explain her calmness in the face of adversity:

> We lived … rent free, you know, we were squatting and I just remember that my mother let me paint on the walls, I was allowed to paint murals and that just did not seem odd to me, but later on I realized that a) most kids are not allowed to paint on the walls, and b) I'd grown up in a world where when disaster is approaching, you don't panic, rather you paint.

Like Adam, whom we discussed in Chapter 4, this appears to make her less prone to the anxieties associated with precarious income. She happily rides the rollercoaster of the postmodern career. Yet her narrative lacks consistency. On the one hand, she proclaims herself to be 'stubborn … single minded' but, on the other, claims to be easily diverted when new opportunities present themselves:

> Like many creative people, I do suffer from professional ADD [Attention Deficit Disorder]. If I have to do one thing for too long, I get really bored and can't focus on it anymore, which is another reason why I know I'm unemployable. If I had to go to the same place every day and talk to the same people, I'd go mental.

Amanda is a fully assimilated subject of the portfolio career, but her skittish-ness means she never develops a sense of craft solidarity or belonging to an occupational community. While in the process of multiskilling she becomes a successful 'just-in-time' worker with a healthy income, Amanda exemplifies Sennett's description of the portfolio life: 'keep moving, don't commit your-self, and don't sacrifice' (Sennett, 1999, p. 25; see also McRobbie, 2002a). She is labile labour, fatalistic and risk taking, embracing the vagaries and turbu-lence of the new economy.

> I'm only just realizing now what a gift it is to be convinced of a path, even a crazy path. I have not had a single moment of doubt ever. I've never had to think about what I wanted to do when I grow up.… Yeah and I'm superstitious because I won't buy a diary till I get a job. And that thought fills me with fear, but it's the same sort of fear that you would expect if you were going to go onto a rollercoaster or something like that. It's fear of the unknown, but it's an excited fear.

Amanda exemplifies the promiscuous aspiration of the portfolio worker. She is open to embarking on a 'crazy path' vocationally and is never so wedded to particular vocational goals that she cannot change tack; she is always ready to parlay her skills towards new market opportunities, even if these deflect her from her prior purpose. She is prepared to hedge against adversity and pre-carity by securing multiple sources of income, and is breezily detached from the sense of embeddedness and long-term belonging: 'I'm walking proof that there is money in the arts, but you've got to be able to do more than one thing.' Amanda is a slashie, a 'jack-of-all-trades', and prepared to improvise and to spend her days pitching for work.

Her film-making ambitions remain alive, although in abeyance, with a long-planned documentary that failed to raise sufficient funds through crowd-sourcing. She is anxious to reassure us that her individualism and entrepreneurial success is not a betrayal of her vocation:

> I'm more interested in making money than in making art, but I haven't sold out as a result of that. If I had to rely on any one of my things, I'd be poorer than I am now and bored because it's not enough, and [producing] requires different levels of energy. I love the energy of producing, but I love the energy of writing and the solo focus. I mean, I'm an only child and I play very well by myself.

It would be wrong to see Amanda's choices as constituting a Faustian pact; she has done what she needed to do to join the dots of her portfolio career and to make a living in an inherently volatile and unpredictable field.

> I'm still here and those 12 people that I studied film with are all gone … I'm an awesome producer, I know how to get money out of people and I know how to hire people, which is all you need to be a producer. I mean that's a skill in itself… talent is not the thing that makes us successful, it's stubbornness, an absolute refusal to do anything else other than this … I make six figures. I've been financially secure for a long time, I've raised kids by myself on a freelancer's income as a film-maker and writer and they are two things that you are not meant to make any money doing. And I still don't know what I am going to do in six months.

By internalizing the injunction of vocational restlessness, she remains open to resetting the coordinates of her career at any time, but in the process relinquishes what many of our interviewees would deem the independence that is synonymous with genuine creativity.

> It's not like training to be an athlete or dancer, not one shot at your dream; you get a million shots, it's just a question of whether you fall at the first hurdle or just get up and keep going. So no Plan B, no fall-back position, [you] don't have a parachute.

Conclusion

Creative biographies typically follow a pattern of enchantment and disenchantment (McRobbie, 2002a, 2002b) as youthful symbolic creativity gives way to the sobering realities associated with making a living in competitive creative fields. In this chapter we have argued that habits and values of working life can endure long after the economic arrangements on which they were based disappear. Blue-collar masculinity was built on stable communities of practice and relatively secure work, with traditions of informal learning, craft/industrial solidarity and hostility towards outside (particularly managerial/bureaucratic) forms of scrutiny. Such stability rarely exists under the precarious and unorthodox employment arrangements of the new economy, but traditional masculine bonds are kept alive in the domestic, educational and recreational spaces. They remain part of the backyard and garage cultures of groups of men – fixing cars, pulling things apart and rebuilding them, DIY projects where groups of friends are brought in to help or amateur team sports. The forms of association, the knockabout and laconic masculinities associated with these gatherings, are deeply embedded in the associations of the factory floor and contrast with the flamboyance and self-promotion required of new labour. Far from being the 'disembedded subjects' of reflexive modernity (Beck et al., 1994), many of our male interviewees are encumbered by cultural baggage that works against the achievement of a successful creative career. We have seen how Tony, Matt and Jake value the slow learning and unconditional sharing of skills that exist in communities of practice at sites of formal and informal learning. Douglas rejects the flamboyant 'auteur' individualism that seems to be part of success in the highly competitive design profession. Many of our male interviewees recoiled at the prospect of networking with strangers, and touting credentials at times and places outside working hours. However, Douglas recognized that such performance was necessary for professional advancement. Mahmoud, although more familiar with small enterprise, was apprehensive about the additional level of scrutiny he would have to endure as a design professional. Having seen art as very personal form of expression, he was uncertain about parlaying this into commercial form. Like other male interviewees, he was diffident about diversifying and transferring his skills and ambitions in ways elicited by the volatile structures of the creative industries. The two young women we presented here – along with those we dealt with in Chapter 2, fashion Tanja and music Nada – described themselves as more versatile and responsive to the possibility of becoming the protégée, to being recognized, discovered and to placing their fortunes in the hands of those who act as creative brokers/gatekeepers. While there are other obstacles to women achieving success in creative fields, they appear to be more responsive to the cultural code of career. This is not by any means to suggest that workplace solidarity is the sole province of men. However, the habits associated with the masculine trade and apprenticeship traditions are generally incompatible with postmodern capitalism, where working lives are often fluid, and success based on individualism and enterprise. These dissonances bubbled to the surface in our interviews. They are apparent in the many interviewees' sober reflections on creative training courses, and their early industry experiences describe the collision of values and circumstances – why *who I am* does not dovetail neatly with *who I wish to become*.

Chapter 6

THE JUST-IN-TIME SELF?

> Life can only be understood backwards; but it must be lived forwards.
>
> Soren Kierkegaard (1843, p. 306)

In opening this book we argued that capitalism now flies the banner of creativity, in part because of the increasing importance of intellectual property to corporate prosperity. Companies can no longer rely exclusively on scientific managers to drive innovation, but must look elsewhere for the symbolic and intellectual labour required to make them competitive. In narrow utilitarian terms, the 'creative economy' is simply a project to persuade artists to transfer their skills in commercially viable directions – to abandon the garret for the graphic designer's studio or the copywriter's office. But creativity is more than simply a set of skills. From a romantic perspective, it involves expressing the inner self in symbolic form – through, for example, the quest to produce the masterpiece or the virtuoso performance. In this deeper sense, the creative economy is a bid to conscript workers' cultural, emotional and intellectual energies for post-Fordist work. New capitalism needs more from labour (whether as wage labourers or subcontractors) than 'skill' and obedience.

For workers, long denied any semblance of vocational fulfillment, the idea of creative work appears to hold the promise that they might (a) salvage a modicum of craft satisfaction from the ruins of Taylorism (b) participate in the traditional arts from which they were long excluded or (c) make a living from their cultural/subcultural enthusiasms even where these involve protest and resistance. It is not easy for capitalism to conscript energies that originate in the private, communal and recreational spheres, especially because most available 'creative work' does not satisfy these ludic/craft/bohemian/subcultural ideals. The jobs do not match the passions, nor even the training and skills.

To overcome this reticence, capital must shift the definition of the term 'creativity' – to extend its lexical range – so as to encourage workers to reassign their ambitions, skills and energies in new and unanticipated directions. This relies on the idea that creativity is not simply an intrinsic quality of a task but a product of the discourse surrounding the labour. We can see examples of this vocational alchemy in the ways that certain forms of work have been transformed in recent history. For example, reality television has added glamour and prestige to the humble art of cooking and encouraged more people in the English-speaking world to develop culinary aspirations (cf France, where the tradition of haute cuisine is more long-standing). While in essence the labour of the cook and the master chef is fundamentally the same, the rise of the celebrity chef, with associated branding and merchandising, elite practices of gourmet consumption and connoisseurship and rating systems like Michelin stars, has given cooking the cachet of a creative career. Today there are occupations – home decorating, hairdressing and gardening – that can be spun either as creative professions or routine manual tasks, depending on the context in which they are framed (Lovink and Rossiter, 2007). There is a sense of vocational possibility associated with creative expression; today, subcultural pursuits are taken into adulthood (Bennett and Hodkinson, 2012) as well as careers (Davis, 2012). Yet as we suggested in the previous chapter, with reference to Douglas, the sheet-metal worker-turned-designer, and other interviewees, many of those from working-class backgrounds, particularly men, find it hard to practice the individualism, self-promotion and entrepreneurial competition associated with the creative career. They take an artisanal view of their work and do not take the creative enchantment of labour seriously. Additionally, even in fields newly sprinkled with the fairy dust of creativity, occupational hierarchies can be steep. Most work on the low-paid, precarious margins in what appear to be day jobs rather than creative jobs.

Promiscuous Ambition? Creativity and the Challenge of Reinvention

For creative aspirants, the experience of training and early working life can be sobering and confronting. Most are forced to redefine their aspirations in the face of adversity. As we have seen, this is especially the case for those who lack the resources to keep them afloat until the career break comes along. The 'logic' of the market suggests that such people must compromise, recalibrate ambition and move into less competitive fields. But the idea of the biographical U-turn can be hard to stomach because of the regret of unfulfilled dreams. But if workers view their creativity – their skills and passions – in abstract terms, then they are more likely to demonstrate the sort of promiscuous ambition required by new capitalism. This extended version of creativity can provide workers with a narrative bridge between discrete and diverse labour-market experiences; to assimilate them to the experience of labour-market churn. Although they lack complete control over their fate, the abstract creative self can exercise *improvised agency* and retain a sense of vocational momentum in the face of shrinking options. To be able to tell a coherent narrative of working life – to yourself and to others – is to communicate the appearance that you have at least some control over your fate, that you are not just tossed around by circumstance. This involves joining the dots in retrospect, connecting 'what I set out to do' with 'the way things have turned out': reconciling erstwhile ambition with life circumstances and embedding (Cunningham, 1998) their creative skills and energies in unusual places (although this may offend creative workers' sense of independence and nonconformity). Creative workers should thus calibrate aspiration around the accumulation of experience and residual vocational identity.

In the remainder of this chapter we will consider the success of this project to reconfigure labour power: what forms of compromise can workers make when erstwhile ambition meets adverse circumstance? Here there are clear struggles and dissonances associated with the nonconformist traditions associated with various forms of creativity – bohemian, subcultural, and craft independence, each of which offer particular protests to capitalism's commodification. There are also, as we saw in the previous chapter, impulses associated with working-class masculinity – in particular – that militate against the creative dissimulations required of the portfolio worker.

John at the junction

We met John in Chapter 2: he was the alienated youth whose teachers had encouraged him to take up the guitar. Undeterred by the derision of fellow students in the working-class school – where sporting achievement was valued more than creative pursuits – he continued playing in the band he had formed with his friends after they left formal education. Having had his musical ambitions kindled during school years, John took risks, investing time and resources in an uncertain creative future. Achieving only poor final high-school results, at first he drifted reluctantly into low-paid manual work in a noisy factory where he could listen to music through his headphones to escape the shift-work tedium and disappear into his rock and roll dreams. Outside work he found time to write music and practice with the band that had been formed at school:

> And I said to them after a year, like, I want to up it, write my own stuff, see if we could get some gigs. So we got all that sorted. And this guy who I worked with I looked up to because he was out there doing it. He gave me a crash course on how to approach agents and venues, what we need to do to approach them. Bounced things off him for a couple of months and then started doing things for myself.

When he told his parents, they were resolutely opposed to the move: 'Music for them was not a career choice. It's fun.' They were sceptical that John could make a living out of it:

> They were against the music thing … Mum and Dad were never risk takers. They always played it by the books and if there wasn't enough money for anything we'd just go without. They still don't take risks.

As many other rock and roll hopefuls have found, achieving success is not easy and John was soon working on commission for a music-booking agency to supplement the meagre returns from live performance. The rewards were minimal and payments were often delayed and he eventually set up his own small booking agency that became his major source of income, but which required enormous effort for little reward. Earning a precarious income on the edges of the music industry (he books small artists to small venues), John told us he is considering getting out. This coincided with a dawning awareness that the career as a musician is out of reach:

> I wanted to be a rock star when I was 17. I still had ambitions of being a rock star until I was like 24 and then I just went 'Nah! It's not gonna hap-pen'… there's a lot of musicians who are more talented than me. So … it's alright … I probably started too late. I wasn't out there soon enough. I made the wrong choice of band members and I was too scared to get away from those guys. … I'm not saying I'm a really good musician, but when it comes to these two guys, they were adequate but they didn't have the drive and they were holding me back, well … holding me back from what [in a tone of sardonic resignation]? From being a booking agent!

At this point in our conversation John almost appears scornful of himself. The dreams have collapsed and the fallback job was scant consolation. He is a long way from being the accomplished, confident, 'just-in-time' worker, ready to see coherence and meaning amongst disparate experiences and forms of work. Instead, John expresses a sense of frustrated ambition. The non-creative 'tread-water' work he was doing until the big break came along had come to define him. It became his vocation by default, neither fulfilling nor lucrative.

The idea of the creative career is based, in part, on this narrative conceit. To be seen as worthy, the aspirant must be willing and able to compose a plausible and unified vocational story. However powerless they might feel in the face of precariousness and vague contingency, they must lay claim to some agency and direction, or at least be prepared to spin the fragments as part of a larger fatal plot, wrought by the confluence of talent and serendipitous circumstance. In this sense then, the postmodern career is little more than an artefact of narrative: if it cannot be narrated it does not exist. And where once such narratives were only performed in limited settings – the job interview, or perhaps when meeting someone who was a gatekeeper in your field – in the 'always-working' world they must now always be on tap. This story must be practised and you must be ready to tell it – of the triumphant unfolding of opportunity and realization of talent – in various face-to-face encounters and, importantly, through social media posts as you curate the public image, the simulacrum of your public self.

In his early thirties when we interviewed him, John had reached the point in life where he felt the need to achieve more stability and is more amenable than many others we interviewed to reflecting on the decisions he has made in pursuit of creative success. He contrasts his choices with those of a younger brother, the most academically successful of his siblings and the only one in his family to attend university:

> So he did four or five years of uni and came out and realized that he can only get a job that pays 45,000 bucks a year. … He did law and marketing. He didn't want to go into the legal field and he went into marketing. Now he's the marketing coordinator [for a fibro cement company] and it's bizarre. He's talking about … fibro cement and I'm like, 'You actually enjoy fibro cement? Why do you want to work in fibro cement?' And he goes, 'It's really exciting. It's got these uses.'

This is a powerful allegory of the limits of aspiration. John's bohemianism and nonconformity might have led to a precarious life but at least his soul has not been conscripted; at least he is not forced to parrot his employer's marketing spiel to rationalize a long period of tertiary study and incurring debt. Here, John is not disparaging higher education itself, but demonstrating his conviction that even the conventional lines of social mobility guarantee neither fulfilment nor a radical break with the parent culture, either in financial or cultural terms. Incremental mobility through conformity is not worth the effort and John finds the way his brother transferred his skills – putting them at the service of selling building materials – less than plausible.

The research interview provided John with a space – perhaps even a therapeutic one – for reflexivity and rumination on how mundane labour overtook creativity and treasured ambition. His no-nonsense working-class persona prevented him from applying teleological gloss to an unwanted vocational transition. While the new economy discourse might construct performer and agent as part the same industry, John realizes that this is nothing more than smoke and mirrors. He reached this point of reckoning as he was contemplating home ownership, marriage and fatherhood:

> Just recently I've been thinking about getting out. It's been seven years it's been great. Yeah. The constant financial stress. There's no guarantees. Like with the venues … they can be there one week and literally the next week they can be gone. … I'm just about to take on a mortgage as well. So it's like I've got the payments each week. Like with the industry being what it is, I don't know what it'll be like in six months. It could increase … If I had to take a punt I'd say it would decrease and that's why I'm getting out. I haven't got any qualifications in anything else.

He has come to recognize that working with in what he calls 'corporate land' will free him from the treadmill of his booking agency, but consign him to even less fulfilling work. With his parents' admonitions ringing in his ears, their desire for him to find 'steady work' like his brother, he faces the challenge of identifying the transferability of his skills and reinventing himself. But he resists acquiescing to their view of working life – accepting that they were 'right all along'.

John's cantankerousness and nonconformity shows through, as demonstrated in his scorn for his brother's corporate career. He discusses the prospect of finding a mainstream job working to someone else's agenda, but demonstrates a great reluctance to do so:

> People are saying I might be able to do project management coordination … I thought if I'm going to make a change I shouldn't do something totally different … something that would use my skill sets. Like I don't work well working for someone else. I always piss my bosses off, always have. So I've got to find something where I can run my own show, have control over deadlines and budgets, otherwise I'll just end up fighting with the boss.

> **Q –** Are you sad about throwing it in?
> **J –** I am. But … I gotta think like what have I got to do about the mortgage payments.

Unable to find the silver linings in the vocational clouds, it is difficult for John to account for these life transitions in positive terms. He bears little resemblance to the versatile and adaptable new worker, and although the pressure to find steady and better paid work may force him to adopt this persona, this simply masks the hidden injuries of the creative class.

Nada on the rebound

We met music industry ingénue Nada in Chapter 3 and learned about her short-lived career in the music industry. She endured humiliating scrutiny of the way she presented herself and, like the central character in the movie *The Devil Wears Prada*, her employer's insistence that she remake her image to fit style and lifestyle norms associated with her job. To become the networking, entrepreneurial music-industry up-and-comer, she would have to wear the right clothes, eat the right food and speak the right way. But such a transformation would alienate her from her Palestinian immigrant family – factory-worker father and nurse mother – a symbolic burning of the bridges with family and community. For Nada, this was too high a price to pay for the chance at a creative career. So scorched was she by this experience that she walked away and cultivated very different ambitions. When we spoke, she was studying psychology at university – her second spell as a student following an abortive enrolment in a science degree after leaving school – and trying to balance the models for working life provided by her parents with the recognition that skills and patterns of work had changed profoundly.

In discussing vocational aspirations, Nada spoke of her father in allegorical terms. He was a long-term worker for a company that produced car parts for large Australian manufacturers until it was bought out by a Japanese company that has taken the business offshore. Having worked his way from the shop floor to a minor supervisory role, but without qualifications, Nada's father faced the prospect of long-term redundancy – a casualty of deindustrialization. Nada lamented his plight:

> He's not ready to retire. And, even if he was, he still wouldn't know what to do with himself … He's done the … 3 p.m. to 3 a.m. shift for 35 years … Yeah, he's more sullen than angry at the moment. He used to be angry. It's been looming over his head for the last five years since the company was bought out.

Nada recalls the sort of vocational advice she received in her youth:

> It was about having a good job and being in the same company for how long and reaping the benefits of being loyal to your workplace. … He used to think that that was how you held a good job. Now that he's at the

other end of it, he's realized that he should have looked for another job earlier on. Or he should've … he wished, he always said he wished he had a trade as a mechanic. Because then if he falls out of work he could become a mechanic on the side. Or, become a carpenter. But because he doesn't have a trade, or something tangible, he doesn't have work.

Nada's sister conformed to the model of 'steady work' by taking a job in a department store, and her parents were proud of her:

So, she's been there for about five years. But my Dad sees that as a much more respectable and stable job. Because it's … a big company, and it won't go bankrupt, and she won't become redundant.[1]

Nada had been the more academically successful and her parents were proud when she won a place in university on leaving school but perplexed as to where a science degree would lead:

He still couldn't understand what I wanted to do, unless it was to become a doctor, or become a nurse. He had to know the occupation to understand.

Nada's parents were dismayed and humiliated when she dropped out:

And in my way I wanted to find that honourable job … In a Middle Eastern culture the kids are corsages on their parents' jackets. They are. I don't agree with it, but for the sake of my parents … How do [my parents] go to their [extended] family, who I know are so judgemental, and say, 'My daughter's dropped out of uni'? I mean, most families would be like, 'Oh, that's alright, she'll find a nice career.' But in a Middle Eastern family it's, 'Oh! That's horrible', and as soon as the back's turned you know exactly what's said about you.

They were further estranged when Nada went to work in the music industry, especially when she began to change, to compromise in order to fit into the creative scene. When she eventually renounced that path it was out of a desire to honor some communal values. But it was a complex process to recover lost ground:

---

1 Ironically in 2016 the company announced closure of several of its stores.

> When I told her I wanted to go back to uni [Mum] said, 'Forget it. You're getting old. You're going to study for another four years and when are you going to start a life, and start a career? And buy your own house...'
>
> **Q –** So, you've had to really work against the grain here. I mean, to actually see yourself through.
>
> **N –** My parents have essentially washed their hands of me, careerwise. They just hope that whatever decision I make doesn't come back to bite me. ... And it's kinda like, 'Look, if you make a wrong decision, you're on your own.'

While wanting to make them proud of her, Nada resists her parents' twentieth-century interpretation of working life: education and work as separate and sequential aspects of the life course, and education institutions supplying gilt-edged and durable vocational qualifications. A psychology degree does not supply a familiar occupational label that can be shared communally. Nor does it appear to offer a solid career path.

> He still thinks it's a waste of time. I should go get a trade or something, I should become a hairdresser, or a secretary or something.

However, at a certain level, the idea of working as a psychologist at least appears as a solid and identifiable vocation. Her father's experiences are salutary for Nada – education and qualifications are important – but the lessons she draws from those experiences are different from those that he draws. Like most young people in the knowledge/creative economy, Nada is flying blind, unsure whether she can make a living as a psychologist, but knowing that twentieth-century vocational stability has all but disappeared.

Temping Tanja

In Chapter 3 we discussed Tanja and her experiences of working in the fashion industry. When she first got the job, she sought advice from more experienced co-workers on how to build a career. They advised her:

> 'Don't stick around because you need to meet new people' and it is all that social networking especially in the fashion industry ... so the more you are out and about and you are changing jobs going from here to there, the more people you are meeting, and the more networking you are doing and the bigger jobs you can land. But the jobs only go for a specific amount of time.

She learnt that, in order to be successful, the new worker has to embrace pre-cariousness. In some industries there is even a formula. Another interviewee, a young recruit to new media/advertising, indicated that three years is widely accepted as the right length of time to remain in one job: not too short so future employers suspect that you are flighty and unreliable, or that you were released by a previous employer once they became aware that your skills and performance were inadequate; but not too long so that you become 'stale' and taken for granted.

After working in the position for two years, Tanja decided the prospect of compulsory vocational restlessness was not to her liking. She also became aware that people employed in positions similar to her own were almost exclusively young. This sharpened the sense of having a short shelf life:

> I think working in the fashion industry it has just really it is not very secure and there is a lot of it is a young job, like a lot of young people, like once you are in your thirties if you don't own your own little company you are not really sort of [secure].

She recognized that those who were successful in the fashion industry had entrepreneurial inclinations, and embraced the challenge of networking and self-promotion.

As we saw in Chapter 3, Tanja was not at ease with the competitive individualism of the fashion world, and so revived her earlier ambition and enrolled in a teacher-education course. She thought this would give her a point of anchorage against a tendency to become captivated by every sparkling opportunity that presented itself. Teaching would give her some control over her working life, the chance to avoid the fate of a fragmented and disparate precarious career. Far from being the sovereign, strategic and versatile new-economy worker, Tanja characterized herself as easily wooed by the flattery of serendipitous opportunity, using the vocabulary of the romance narrative:

> I need something that is a little bit more stable I think, because I just get swept off ... on a tangent and fall in love with something else.

However, she also presented her impulsiveness as a virtue. These qualities, she suggested, give her the disposition to be a versatile teacher, to bring a range of skills that will give her a role beyond the classroom:

> I want to be involved in a lot of things within the school because just being a teacher in the classroom would drive me insane, like I need to be

doing different things like organizing you know the dance, or you know running cross country or I need to be doing different things all the time.

Tanja can see the virtue of a job that has many aspects, and that can accommodate her diverse enthusiasms. However, it provides a point of anchorage, a core vocational identity, one that does not require her to engage in the labour of professional reproduction, the pressure to renew and reinvent herself according to the rhythms of the postmodern career. It gives her the ability to plan and anticipate that is not available for most who work in creative industries.

Conclusion

We presented these cases here because they are people who have reached a point of reckoning in their lives, of interrupted momentum, where they no longer enjoy the aspirant's wide-eyed optimism and openness, where structural forces of various sorts have dashed or dampened their creative dreams. Nada and John reached this point by age thirty. Nada's coruscating foray into the music industry threw up a dilemma. When her employer demanded that she present herself through some contrivance of inner-city cool, she correctly understood that this would involve the symbolic abandonment of family and community. This was too large a sacrifice. So she sought alternatives by which she could avoid the demeaning pressure to remake her image and still achieve social mobility. Nada's parents found it hard to fathom her job with a digital music company, yet, while she was keen to make them proud, they remained perplexed by her decision to study psychology. Like many working-class people, they viewed university study as primarily for obtaining durable skills and vocational credentials. Her choice appeared vague and precarious, a gamble they did not support and for which she alone would live with the consequences. John reached the creative reckoning in a different way: at the point where he needed a steady income to buy a house and have a family. As a musician and performer he understood and was loyal to the protest culture and rough vernacular of rock and roll, and to the blunt honesty of his working-class roots, which provided little space to perform and dissimulate a creative career. For John, creativity could not be dissimulated; it is not an artefact of discourse but a grounded process. For Tanja, the initial excitement working in a fashion career gave way to a sober realization that its turbulence and precarity were not for her. Rather than subject herself to the arbitrary and fickle evaluations of the industry gatekeepers, to all the uncertainties of life in the gig economy, she doubled back and sought something less glamorous but more reliable. While, at a certain level, she was more sanguine about the change of direction than many other interviewees – teaching would accommodate her character traits, such as being artistic and drawn to diverse interests – she certainly did not present the transition as seamless. Rather, the experience in fashion was salutary and one from which she wanted to move on.

Chapter 7

BEYOND THE SOCIAL FACTORY: RECLAIMING THE COMMONS

To recap, we have argued that behind the rhetoric of the creative economy is a neo-liberal project to transform labour. This has several elements: to habituate workers to new capitalism's churn and upheaval; to encourage them to be optimistic despite their experience of precarity, underemployment and professional/career abeyance; and to persuade them to be ready to transfer their creative skills, passions and ambitions towards the opportunities the market presents. In the creative economy, workers should give up on any expectation of a steady, long-term job, and instead look at working life as a series of gigs. The increasing influence of globalization and digitization over economic processes, and the weakening of industrial rights, have undermined job stability. So companies expect workers to be flexible and biddable. In one sense they must live like artists – hand-to-mouth – and be ready to bring the same creative energies to work that they apply to their art, even when performing routinized and low-skilled tasks. But in another sense, they must relinquish the artist's suspicion of commercialization. This chapter will consider how capitalism meets this latter challenge – how it brings creativity to market. Following Boltanski and Chiapello (2006), we argue that the system's remarkable durability is in part based on its capacity to absorb critique. Modern capitalism's alienated labour, mass production and consumption provoked various forms of popular resistance, including from artistic, subcultural and countercultural communities. The popularity of the idea of creative work rests in its implicit promise to remedy these ills, and free us from lives of rigid industrial direction.

However, as we have seen, the task of yoking art to enterprise is not straightforward. In this chapter we look at the idea of the social factory in more detail and how it challenges the work/play binary. In one sense, immaterial labour is everywhere, but, from a neoclassical economic perspective, it is not *productive labour* until it is harnessed for profit. So how to make it productive? Immaterial labour rarely complies with the rigid directions and techniques of scientific management. So employers must use a variety of techniques to make their workers feel at home and to draw out the sorts of cultural and emotional energies that traditional workers rarely brought to the workplace, and conserved for pleasurable private and communal practices. This means disguising the work environment as something else to bring out the emotions and creative dispositions that are generally reserved for the private realm. However, new capitalism has fewer and fewer workers, in the traditional sense of wage labourers, as it relies on outsourcing work to small producers/contractors under post-Fordist arrangements. We consider how creative people navigate and rationalize the process of becoming entrepreneurs – especially the radicals, nonconformists and outsiders – and ask what the cultural means are by which they do this. We use the term 'feral enterprise', to capture a variety of entrepreneurial activities that bear little resemblance – and in some cases stand in opposition – to modern capitalism. Small creative entrepreneurs often seek to conserve the integrity of their art, but this commitment generally does little to alleviate their economic vulnerability. In concluding the chapter we will look at what forms of social, financial and institutional support are required for the as-yet-unrealized project of creative renewal: alternatives to the neo-liberal utopian fantasy that small enterprise will be the engine of future prosperity. In particular, we will consider how universities can play a central role in this process.

Herding Cats –'Value-Capture' in the Social Factory

It is now commonplace to observe that symbols and knowledge have increasing economic importance, and that we must broaden our understanding of production to include immaterial as well as material processes. While material production is constrained by geography – manufacturing occurs in particular places – immaterial production appears to be less so. The concept of the social factory recognizes that the latter can be widely dispersed (although ironically, as we observed in Chapter 3, it rarely is), especially in the era of digital communication, but it also points to a paradox in the idea of production itself. If creativity exists as recreation prior to being conscripted as labour, at what point does it become productive? The idea of the social factory suggests the possibility of bridging the public/private work/play binaries that were central to modern society.

The concept also requires that we rethink the production and consumption divide. Modern capitalism treated consumers as essentially passive and sought to engineer their choice design and marketing techniques and so forth. It was also based on the idea that the manufacturer could determine the cultural meaning of a commodity, and the way it was consumed. But post-Fordist capitalism recognizes what cultural theorists have long known (Hall, 1980; Harney, 2010): that consumption is much more active and can defy the hubris of marketing. This can be seen most obviously in the youth cultures – music, clothing and so forth – where the rapid turnover of styles follows the erratic rhythms and registers of cool, subcultural distinction and so forth, and where, through processes of bricolage – cultural resignification – the meanings that consumers attach to commodities can be completely at odds with the producers' intentions (e.g. as Dick Hebdidge (1979) observed, when punks used safety pins and dog collars as jewellry). The concept of the social factory suggests not only that fashion is volatile and difficult to track and marshal, but that production doesn't end at the point it is sold. Shorthose goes so far as to claim that 'the act of *consumption* becomes the moment of production' (Shorthose, 2004, p. 3). To extend the concept of production to include the *production of meaning* – to see consumers as producers – prompts a rethink of the whole idea of labour. Labour, in this wider sense, is everywhere and market competitiveness depends on being able to tap the dispersed cultural practices and immaterial resources that circulate in the private, communal and recreational realms.

So how does capital herd these cats of creativity? The Fordist approach treats labour as two-dimensional and manipulable through the techniques of scientific management. The formula appears relatively simple (though it's rarely so simple in execution): the worker travels from home to work, and performs tasks obediently under managerial direction. Managers, not workers, drive productive innovation. But the sorts of creativity now required from workers thrive in less formal and regimented conditions, and are tied to emotions and impulses culturally grounded outside of employment. So to persuade them to give up their creative secrets means breaking down the work/play division that is central to the social psychology of modern life. By contrast with Taylorism's treatment of workers as machine-minders, as adjuncts to technological processes designed by others, new capitalism talks not only about fostering talent and job satisfaction, and encouraging the idiosyncratic traits that might once have marked employees as unsuitable. The geeks, artists and mavericks may appear strange, but they are capable of insights that can generate great wealth, and they must be encouraged to bring their quirkiness to work. (Nobody saw Bob Dylan or Mark Zuckerberg coming!)

So companies seek to harvest the creative bounty by camouflaging the workplace. This is most obvious in the Silicon Valley heartlands, where companies like Apple, Google and Microsoft build *campuses* not offices, as youthful corporate leaders, some of whom made their discoveries at university, try to recreate both the anarchic spirit of radical experimentation and the ludic aspects of the undergraduate environment. There are rooms for meditation, playing music, table tennis or online games. You can role-play with colleagues, or sit and doodle in a corner, just so long as you are plugged in when inspiration strikes. Artists and 'futurists' are employed as motivational speakers at staff retreats, encouraging employees to think outside the square, to rinse the psychological residue of Fordism from labour. Montessori management replaces the time-and-motion enslavement of skill to process, conception and execution. However, despite the appearance of modernizing and humanizing work, none of this involves a break with existing arrangements: profits remain paramount.

It is not just the corporate unicorns, the trailblazers of digital capitalism, that seek to disguise their workplaces and lull their employees into thinking they are somewhere else. Retailers also try tricks like this, as we saw in Chapter 4 when looking at the experiences of surfer Anne, whose employers tried to conscript her youth-cultural skills to sell their clothing. They try to disguise customer relations as breezy and informal peer interaction, and the shop as a meeting place rather than a point of sale (Zwick and Cayla, 2011). This goes deeper than just an attempt to capture workers' 'aesthetic skills' (Warhurst and Nickson, 2001); it is about persuading people like Anne to bring her subcultural persona to work.[1] You may not be able to trap and bottle all of the dispersed forms of creativity, but you can try to simulate the environment in which it thrives.

---

1 Chain restaurants now often seek creative skills amongst their recruits. Subway advertised for 'sandwich artists': https://www.mysubwaycareer.com/Home/JobDescriptions?clt=en-CA. And McDonalds used 'Delaney's Story' (https://mcdonalds.com.au/learn/careers#/) to suggest that service amounts to a dramaturgical encounter!

Similar techniques are employed in some areas of hospitality, where companies try to evoke domesticity and to bring the feelings and emotional investments among their workers that are usually reserved for family life. The photograph above shows a recruitment advertisement in the window of a coffee-and-pastry chain outlet in Sydney. It advertises not for workers but for 'housemates'. The company website states that it seeks to 'recreate what home feels like – comfortable, cozy, relaxing, flawed, unquestionably accepting, eclectic and sweet'. Thus they seek to sublimate the cold sales transaction with a gift relationship; to replace commerce with nurture and comfort. By creating the sense that the space is welcoming and homely, that you can 'be yourself', the company reasons that their workers will be more likely to work hard, and that customers will consume more. This is a larger project to break down their 'day-job' disposition, to encourage them to bring habits and emotions to the workplace that are more characteristic of private life (Hochschild, 2003). But as we have seen, and as the example of Anne illustrates, workers are often hostile to this sort of social engineering and incorporation in its various forms.

Feral Enterprise

We have considered how companies try to harvest employee creativity, but in the new economy the traditional employment contract is becoming less and less common. Much creative industry work is performed outside the wage relation under post-Fordist arrangements in which large companies subcontract to small firms tasks that might once have been performed in house. This provides the former with greater labour flexibility and transfers to the latter the burden of reproducing themselves in professional terms. Such reproduction includes (a) keeping their skills up to date by funding their own training (b) organizing to insure themselves against being unable to work and (c) covering all the overheads and responsibilities of running a business, including the costs of a workspace.

The studios, workshops and offices of the social factory can take several forms. They are often small spaces that bear little resemblance to the corporate office or factory. Microentrepreneurs frequently work from home or in small rented offices, including in the commercial co-work spaces that are proliferating in metropolitan centres around the world. Many of these are designed to be informal, to make those who work there feel at home, and also – with cafes and communal spaces – to encourage networking. They attract tenants partly by creating the impression that they are incubators of new capitalism, hubs of contacts and projects.

The decision to incorporate – to set up a business to sell their wares – is often not a natural transition for creative aspirants, especially those for whom creativity is rooted in protest culture, in challenging moral conservatism and mainstream consumption. It can also pose an existential challenge to those who come from

Spaces Co-Work Centre Amsterdam

the traditional arts. Even though such people have traditionally relied on brokers and agents to market their work, they generally remain one step removed from the commercialization of their work. So there is a need for some sort of ethical grounding for small creative enterprise, cultural and philosophical resources to allow creatives to distinguish between good and bad capitalism. It is not simply the scale of the enterprise that determines its integrity – though this is clearly part of it – it is that many small entrepreneurs need a grounding mythology, a way of validating some forms of business, while deriding others.

The myth[2] of feral enterprise provides a source of such a rationalization – describing an acceptable version of capitalism that purports to be faithful to the resistant, craft, bohemian and/or iconoclastic values of creativity. It describes a seamless transition from youthful free play and experimentation to the artisanal production and marketing of commodities and services that are sourced from ludic/artistic/subcultural milieus. The various versions of the myth of feral enterprise are usually anti-individualistic, celebrating the collective origins of a business: describing the coming together of those who founded the company around shared cultural enthusiasm. The entrepreneurs must avow a continuing loyalty to the larger field of collective cultural practice in order to distinguish themselves from the moguls of transnational capitalism: the venal and rapacious figures who dwell in the shadows, rip off the artists and small producers and strip them of their intellectual property. The feral enterprise myth provides a narrative bridge between non-market symbolic practices and small entrepreneurship, describing a route from art to enterprise that avoids abhorrent corporate compromise and conserves the values rooted in pre-existing lifestyles and cultures. It confers a gloss of authenticity to small production and aligns it with a growing popular critique of global capitalism. It can also provide the raw material with which to recalibrate ambition, to hold together the dwindling biographical narrative of artist and creative worker with that of creative entrepreneur. Feral enterprise represents a cultural hook for young people navigating the transition to adulthood.

All of this is consistent with the idea of the social factory: you are both a fan and a producer; your work is just an extension of some other part of your life; your customers are your peers. If you can maintain this symbiosis – the *call and response* of the cultural scene – then it becomes legitimate to market your work. As Sarah Thornton observes, 'DJs, club organizers, clothes designers, music and style journalists and various record industry professionals all make a living from their subcultural capital' (1995) p. 203. In her study of hip-hop performers who become cultural entrepreneurs, Laura Speers (2015) observes that her interviewees do not see themselves as fundamentally distanced from the genre's participatory culture. While commercial rap might foster fame dreams, there is also a sense, even at this level, that performers come from and retain strong bonds with the subcultural scenes from which they came. A similar sense that organic communal connections can provide ethical legitimacy to business activities can be identified amongst small lifestyle/craft entrepreneurs. Susan Luckman (2015, 2016) shows that many of those who try to make a living from their craftwork are seeking a better work-life balance and more fulfilling and

---

2 We use myth in the anthropological sense to refer to a narrative that gives meaning and coherence to a way of life – rationalizing particular social arrangements, values and customs. Its significance is more cultural than empirical.

less alienated work. Craft production meets a need for ethical consumption in setting up businesses to supply those markets, largely through craft/maker websites like Etsy, which tell prospective customers the vendors' stories and endeavour to forge social bonds in order to soften and humanize the commodity relationship. Luckman draws on Ekinsmyth's (2013) term 'mumpreneurs', referring to those who engage in small-scale business associated with the labour of reproduction. The persona of motherhood is prioritized over the competitive entrepreneurial drive. The business is ostensibly incidental to the craft and the emotions, experience and relationships that spawned it.

Case Study: Rebel8

REBEL 8

The Rebel8 logo

Vivid Festival 2014, Sydney 'On Collaboration, Commerce and Credibility in Youth Culture' Mikey Giant and Joshy G – Keynote

Rebel8, an American company based in California that manufactures casual clothing and accessories based on a street art/skateboarding aesthetic, exemplifies the myth of feral enterprise. Founded by tattooist Mike Giant, and Joshy G, a graffiti artist, the company describes itself as 'deeply rooted' in those subcultures. The sense of brotherhood between these two men is central to the company's founding narrative: an organic friendship developed between the two after they met in the late nineties. Micke tattooed the HiFi Art logo on Joshy D's arm and they become brothers/partners – a symbolic coming together through the skin. The tattoo represents a radical refusal of the idea of transition, a mark of youthful defiance, rejecting the scripted conformity of adulthood. The enterprise was founded as a modest project when in 2003, 'with just $500, Joshy printed a small run of tees and sold them out of a messenger bag around the city. REBEL8 was born' (http://rebel8.com/pages/history). This story evokes their street-based credentials, symbolically connecting with members of the mobile urban subcultures to whom they seek to market their goods.

Giant and Joshy D founders of Rebel8

This photograph shows them sitting on the back of a truck like vintage clothing merchants at a street stall. They have become successful large entrepreneurs but they continue to project the image of small trade. They blog their daily lives so as to communicate their ordinariness, and there are images of graffiti art on walls and in galleries, demonstrating that they are concerned not just with commodified designs but with aesthetics.

The idea of the social factory involves blurring the line between producers and consumers, disguising the commodity relationship as something other than it is. This comes through when Joshy discusses the experience of being asked to sign autographs at Rebel8 events:

> I like to think of my autographs as the periods on kool conversations that just went down. I love to engage fans and not only tell my story, but listen to theirs as well. REBEL8 has always been and still remains a personal passion project that you're a key part of. (http://rebel8.com/blogs/news?page=4)

The conversation is a sense of co-production, collaboration, the challenge to the idea of the 'artist-auteur', suggesting the idea of consumers as proto-producers. Mike and Joshy blog about the random neo-tribal encounters that the Rebel8 sign can give rise to:

> I love that […] I'm 42 years old and I'm still in this cool culture where we still go talk to each other, we find each other in the midst of the soup of humanity, you see one across the street and say 'Hey he's got a huge eight on his shirt! Who's that? Let's go talk to him.' (http://rebel8.com/blogs/news?page=4)

This suggests that the brand functions as symbolic recognition – the emblem by which the dispersed members of a neo-tribe can find each other. Thus the t-shirts and baseball caps are not simply commodities. Rather, they serve a constructive communal purpose: to break down the anonymity and social isolation of contemporary cities.

A key element of the myth of feral enterprise is expressed here: that enterprise and work can be *ludic*, rather than simply concerned with alienated work. Rebel8 trades on the impression that the business has emerged from the pre-existing subculture, to which it remains organically connected and thus the profit motive is incidental to proselytizing the values and aesthetics associated with the scene. They reproduce the resistant and cryptic motifs that, for the most part, only the subculture cognoscenti can read. Rebel8 are careful to give the impression that they embrace artisanal values and production methods and reject mainstream commercial youth culture. They offer a model of capitalism under which you can stay in control of your operations and avoid 'selling out': being co-opted by transnational cultural corporations. Most importantly, Joshy D and Mike Giant suggest that creative entrepreneurs can sidestep 'social ageing' – job, mortgage, conventional suburban life – and keep practising a youthful way of life. Feral enterprise is a way of avoiding the sorts of stark choices we described earlier in this chapter: they were never forced to make a career out of their day jobs or to allow their emotions, imagination and symbolic creativity to be hijacked by big capitalism.

The Rebel8 narrative is typical of the myth of feral enterprise that informs vocational choices and shapes labour market patterns in ways that defy economic rationalist logic. This myth gains traction in the hinge moments, where the challenge to articulate a coherent biographical narrative is most pressing, but where the transition to adulthood remains confusing/formidable. It operates retroactively, weaving subcultural enthusiasm into the narrative of the improvised postmodern career. Youth are thus depicted as proto-subcultural entrepreneurs.

Digital Insurgents

The idea of feral enterprise appears useful not just to categorize craft, artistic and subcultural business but also much of what goes on in the digital start-up economy. In his book *From Counter-Culture to Cyber-Culture* Turner (2006) argued that the early dot com entrepreneurs were steeped in protest cultures, libertarianism and bohemian nonconformity; that they saw themselves as challenging the business and political establishment. Douglas Williams (2015) identifies a similar outsider sensibility in his recent book *Flat-White Economy*. Here he argues that new capitalism is being led by people who bear little resemblance to the tycoons of the past. Treading lightly on the ground, they renounce the old patterns of conspicuous consumption for a relatively austere, low-carbon lifestyle. They live in small spaces, and often the most expensive things they own are their Macbooks and the bicycles that they prefer to cars for getting around cities. This hipster capitalism is rooted in inner-city subcultures and so draws on social networks that bring artists/bohemians together with those with business and digital skills, often in derelict post-industrial places (Lloyd, 2006), to prospect for intellectual property networks that, as we saw in Chapter 3, tend to exclude those from working-class and minority backgrounds.

Those who embrace this sort of insurgent entrepreneurial ideal are generally suspicious of the overtures of large companies and governments. This can be illustrated by an example from London. In the lead up to the 2012 Olympics, the British government directed energy and resources towards establishing new economy 'incubators'. It targeted a digital hub that had grown up in a low-rent area around the Old Street roundabout – known as Silicon Roundabout, an ironic reference to Silicon Valley for a dreary part of London's East End. Prime Minister David Cameron announced in 2010 that this would be rebadged as Tech City and would become a focus of new economy development. Companies who established there would receive tax credits and tech entrepreneurs with financial backing would be eligible for an entrepreneur visa to establish their businesses in the UK.

Insurgent companies are taking advantage of thousands of new innovations and millions of new consumers to generate billions in revenue
within a matter of years. This is where so much of the promise of new
jobs and opportunities lie and that's why, as part of our strategy for
growth, we've made a really important decision. We're not just going
to back the big businesses of today, we're going to back the big businesses of tomorrow. We are firmly on the side of the high-growth, highly
innovative companies of the future. Don't doubt our ambition. (https://
www.gov.uk/government/speeches/east-end-tech-city-speech)

The process involved persuading transnational digital companies to set up
branch offices in the area with the idea that this would produce something
akin to speed dating between small and large enterprise, between those with
start-up ideas and possible investors – the colonization of the social factory:

For the past few weeks and months, we have had dozens of meetings
with technology companies and venture capital investors from across the
world. We said to them: 'Here's our vision for East London tech city – a
hub that stretches from Shoreditch and Old Street to the Olympic Park.
This is what local businesses are saying they need. What part can you
play in making it happen?'

However, in keeping with the enigmatic and inscrutable character of the social
factory, there emerged a sort of libertarian backlash to these initiatives. The
chief creative officer of Mint Digital – based in the East End – wrote scath-
ingly of the state's intervention, saying that it was in danger of compromising
the insurgent and feral edge of their work:

We don't want a culture of chasing grants and buttering up officials. We
don't particularly want to encourage Facebook or Cisco to set up here. If
they do, that's fine but if they don't, that means less competition for great
talent (the key resource). The cluster has arisen spontaneously. It's at a deli-
cate early stage. It's arrogant for the government to believe that its heavy
hand can help. The best thing the government can do is get out of our hair
and use the money to reduce their funding gap or, if they really want, throw
a big party. Actually, I wouldn't trust a government party. (ZDNet, 2011)

The chief executive of Trampoline Systems, Charles Armstrong, was quoted
as saying:

If Shoreditch becomes a bland neighbourhood of corporations and
chain cafes the flourishing startup scene could be stopped dead in its

tracks. (BBC News, 10 March 2015) (http://www.bbc.co.uk/news/technology-15671829).

These sentiments epitomize the spiky anarchic ethos of new capitalism, resisting both the state hothousing of gentrification and official attempts to superintend the relations of creativity and enterprise that they saw as compromising the edgy post-industrial spaces in which feral enterprise takes root.

The maverick spirit parallels the demonization of the jobsworth in popular culture – the small-minded bureaucrat, the purveyor of petty rules, red tape, and forms of surveillance, the imposer of budget constraints. The jobsworth appears in fiction, film and television as the police inspector who frustrates the efforts of the 'old-school' cop to catch the 'crim'; as the middle manager who cuts money for research that is on the verge of finding a cure for cancer. The folk hero, by contrast, is the one who breaks the rules and stares down officious and petty-minded managers. Such people 'go rogue' and take a risk based on a long shot: the hare-brained hunch of the wayward genius. This derring-do readiness to work without a net, the frontier adventurer's reckless indifference to rules, direction and advice, has become synonymous with hairy-chested entrepreneurialism. Those who dare can make money (or make money for you!); those who conform will die wondering.

There is a deep and powerful irony here: new capitalism recognizes that the very structures upon which professional career advancement depended in the past – slavish obeisance to corporate rules, a narrow book-entry view of the world, a technocrat's small mindedness – might in fact be a hindrance to genuine creative innovation. This reflects a deep existential doubt that is captured in David Graeber's polemical essay 'On the Phenomenon of Bullshit Jobs' (2013). Graeber identifies the strange syndrome whereby those in apparently powerful and prestigious jobs talk of feeling that their work lacks value. Graeber's argument is that so much white-collar work, particularly in the private sector, is socially and culturally meaningless and unproductive in a broad sense. Those who perform this work suspect that both job satisfaction and genuine innovation happen outside of the conventional workplace and the field of managerial vision, in the messy borderlands of work and play. And it is the dark horses who are both creative and fulfilled in this sense: the outsiders, mavericks, artists and geeks. Such people would be out of place in corporate boardrooms or gentlemen's clubs. They do not crave or respect the conventional career, but what they do and what they know is potentially valuable.

Social Factory or Sweatshop?

We can see then that the idea of feral enterprise operates on two levels. Firstly, it serves to provide ethical legitimacy to those who set up as sole traders/

start-ups/ freelancers. It suggests that they can continue to challenge the social privilege and perhaps power of old capitalism. Secondly, it provides conservative policymakers with a sexy ideological rationalization for neo-liberalism. To such people, the creative start-ups, 'permalancers' and sole traders represent the green shoots germinating in the composting remnants of old capitalism. However, there is nothing to suggest that the environment of creative freelancers is any more cooperative and humane than the forms of accumulation that preceded it, that it confers any greater degree of social benefit. Little trickles down and not all the boats are floated by rising tides. Rather, the social factory is individualistic and hypercompetitive.

The vision of the society of entrepreneurs – where the market guarantees individual and collective prosperity – has a long history. It underpinned British Prime Minister Margaret Thatcher's vision to regenerate Britain in the 1980s through the Enterprise Allowance Scheme, which provided people with an alternative (and a less coercive/intrusive) regime of support to the dole. It had the effect of removing them from the unemployment statistics. Similar schemes have been instituted in various parts of the Western world. But of course many of the 'businesses' established under this support were destined to fail, particularly in depressed areas where there were few customers with money. There are only so many personal trainers, mobile beauticians and pet groomers that a post-industrial city can sustain:

> In 1991, fresh out of college and determined to become a writer, I was a recipient of a Government Enterprise Allowance Scheme grant. The scheme was a scam, dreamed up in the Thatcher Administration's dying days, to manipulate unemployment figures by redesignating swaths of jobless people as 'small businesses.' The amount you received was more or less the same as what you got on the dole, but you didn't have to show up at a job center and sign for it, and, vitally, you were no longer classified as unemployed but, rather, as a fledgling enterprise marketing X or Y or Z: gardening or odd-jobbing, hairdressing or massage. Basically, whatever you already did while jobless. To qualify, all you had to do was draw up a 'business plan', whose execution would never be verified. Effectively, it was a fiction. (McCarthy, 2016)

Those creative workers funnelled towards setting up as sole traders in the gig economy model often struggle to make a living. Recent British data (Bounds, 2015) suggests that while there was a spectacular growth in the number of small businesses established after the 2008 global financial crisis, the average income across all such enterprises dropped quite sharply. What conservative politicians vaunt as a small, enterprise-led recovery, is actually a mask for the problems of poverty and precarity that would in an earlier era be manifested in the unemployment data. Many of the subcontracting arrangements that operate in creative fields amount simply to 'arms-length' exploitation of people who are de facto employees, in that they obtain most of their work from a single corporate or institutional source. This is represented in the number of businesses operating in creative fields with no employees. In the UK, for example, 88.7 per cent of businesses in 'motion picture, video and television programme production, sound recording and music publishing activities' and 92.7 per cent in 'creative, arts and entertainment activities' have no employees (Arts Council of England, 2015). This compares with 75.3 per cent of all businesses. However, in recent years, there has been a considerable expansion of the gig economy beyond creative industries – partly through companies like Uber and Deliveroo, who offer bites of work to sole traders.

Scholars are divided in assessing the prospects of those who work in the social factory. Autonomist theorists (Gorz, 1989; Negri, 1989; Lazzarrato, 1996; Virno, 1996; Shorthose, 2004; Marazzi, 2008) claim that it can liberate workers, lead to the formation of a 'creative commons', worker independence, collective institutions and political resistance. Such things can eventually form the basis for challenging big capitalism. Other theorists see the social factory as rescuing labour from the doldrums of alienation and recovering the artisanal way of life. For Lasch (1994), the social factory's informalized work settings have re-traditionalized work relations, recuperating the 'pre-modern and communal-traditional' communities of practice that were dismantled by Taylorism's project of worker alienation. Other commentators are less sanguine, arguing that new capitalism generates a climate of competitive individualism where overwork, exploitation and poverty are the norm (McRobbie, 2002a, 2002b; Pratt and Gill, 2008; Scharff, 2016). Under these circumstances there is little scope for radical alternative worker cooperation and a challenge to unequal social relations. Major companies retain control over production, distribution and profits and retain workers in situations of bondage, albeit outside of the wage relation. De Peuter argues that new capitalism conscripts the energy of independent creativity by collapsing the work life division and developing a 'parasitical relation of the market to the common' (de Peuter 2001). Hesmondhalgh claims that the creative economy is not characterized by a radical break with the past, and that there is 'sufficient continuity to undermine the suggestion that we have entered a new era of cultural production' (2007, p. 260). Feminist writers claim that the allocation of work contracts through informal networks simply magnifies patriarchal power. Additionally, they argue that erratic patterns of work are not compatible family life and caring responsibilities, the burden of which generally falls more on women (Adkins, 1999; Gill, 2002, 2008; Banks and Milestone, 2011).

Some of the difficulties and disappointments of the freelancing life can be illustrated with reference to two of our interviewees, both film-makers and men in their early fifties, and each of whom have reached a point in life of critical reflection on their long-term precarity, and the lack of opportunity to perform creatively fulfilling work.

Stuart: matrimonial auteur

Stuart is from a middle-class background, and attended a wealthy private school. A fan of early kung fu movies – of Jackie Chan and Bruce Lee – he developed ambitions to become a film-maker and took a college course after he left school. After graduating he worked as an audio-visual technician in a government department, something he saw as a stop-gap day job – a step in the path to making feature films:

> VHS operation was my first course, then VHS editing, and then I got a job as an AV technician. … I had a strategy. I knew I wanted to make films, but it's difficult to get into the film industry in Australia because it's small. So I thought it must be easier to get into television. … I thought if I get into TV then it'd be an easy transfer into film. Then to get into television might be hard, so maybe I should get into video and that way I can get into television and then into film.

This vocational strategy did not work and, forced to lower his sights, Stuart started up a wedding video production business. He reflected on this phase of his life in terms consistent with the idea of creative work that we discussed in the previous chapter: he sought to endow what was essentially mundane and generic film work with the patina of enchantment. This came through in the interview when he expressed his quixotic ambition of bringing artistic filmic values to the wedding video. He discussed his impatience with his subjects for their lack of cooperation: they were not actors and they disrupted the creative process rather than collaborating in it; his aims and theirs differed.

> With a [wedding] production you need stars, talent, and you've got that; you need locations, well you've definitely got that; you need wardrobe, well you've definitely got that; you need catering, you've got that with a wedding; and transport, all that sort of stuff. But when you get there on the day, no one cares about you making your video. You're not there to make a video, you're there, or everyone's there, to have a wedding, so they'll do things that totally disregard consideration that we're actually trying to make a video here … so you set your exposure because the church is dark, but when the doors open up there's going to be a big burst of light… so you're ready, they start the music, the door opens up, there's the bride, you start to zoom in and fifteen people get in the aisle

and you can't rush up the aisle kicking people and say get out of the way, you've wrecked my shot, stop the music.

There is pathos in Stuart's frustration at being unable to elevate the form of wedding video into filmic art. He is essentially performing mundane labour, generic work, but when the aesthetic quality of his work is disrupted like this, so too is his artistic sense of self.

Eventually, Stuart realized that the small business was too chancy and precarious, and so he took a job in a school working as an audio-visual technician. With a family to support, the small business was too marginal and precarious wedding videos could not support his family. He makes sense of being unsuited to the grind and graft of selling himself, of networking in a post-Fordist setting, by referring to the division of labour that operates in the film industry:

> So I'm much better at doing the job than getting the job, I'm not that good at selling myself … networking and going out and doing all that stuff, that's the producer's job, I'm more the director, I'm very good at directing.

It was not possible for Stuart to work as a freelancer, even at the creative margins. Although he yearned for a degree of craft autonomy and the chance to express the skills he was trained in, Stuart could not do this as a freelancer/small entrepreneur. Working as an audio-visual technician provided a regular pay packet and the stability needed to support his family.

Mid-life Mike

Also in his fifties, Mike presents as careworn and having lost interest in meeting the demands of the creative career. From a working-class Irish background, he learned to make films after he left school while participating in a 'work-for-the-dole' project. The course required him to participate in a video making course and make a government training video. Later he moved to London, which, in the eighties, was a place of high unemployment and social and political unrest. Mike got a job setting up council-funded media training programs in a local arts centre, for 'at-risk' youth. He enjoyed working with ordinary people much like himself, but, despite this, felt he was 'wiping the arse of Tory Britain, and was part of the apparatus that was just a fuck up'. In his late twenties he migrated to Australia with the aim of making a living as a film-maker.

Initially he worked part time as an AV technician, and fly-posting advertising signs in the evenings ('what a shitty job that is'). For fifteen years he was a jobbing freelancer, living on project funding and continuing to work with young people from marginal communities. He made a number of films that brought him some moderate acclaim, but

> I realized … that I had no saleable skills, and I couldn't carry on in that situation. It's just not viable, and when you've got kids and a mortgage … I suppose the long and the short of it is that film-making on its own isn't going to cut it and isn't ever going to be financially sustainable, and I realized that the only jobs I could go for or the area of work I could get cash money was in production management, which is a shit job, only uses a small amount of my skills and experience and I'd be a cog in the wheel.

Not wishing to be diverted to performing more administrative tasks away from the more fulfilling and creative labour in his field, he needed an alternative source of income. Family responsibility limited Mike's ability to live frugally or precariously, but rather than leaving film-making completely, he enrolled in a post-graduate course on a scholarship, which provided some regular (if meagre) income for three years. This gave him the buffer he needed, and the time to recalibrate his skills, continue to produce films and make money but

> I'm up against these kids coming out of college who work fourteen hours a day and who have probably got more up-to-date computer skills … so one of the big pluses with the [course] is that I could continue to produce stuff, 'cause if I wasn't in a job where I could be creating stuff, I'd probably get frustrated and want to move on.

His words illustrated the contrast between the collective and emancipatory idealism that drew him to film-making in the first place, and the highly individualistic, competitive and precarious conditions under which film-makers worked. He told us the industry is

> … very competitive, working with film-makers who are dysfunctional and narcissistic and completely crazy and who climb over their grandmothers to make a film…. [T]rying to make a living in this low-budget arena is extremely stressful … psychologically punishing … there is no division between your personal life and your professional life, it's all in there in one big, fucking mess, and you're talking about large amounts of money. You're talking [the cost of] a small house or a medium drug deal, you know. It's a fuck of a lot of money to be up for; and if things don't go right, and when you're dealing with those amounts of money, there is always the possibility that things will go down the toilet and then you're fucked.

Mike is weary of the fragile social relations and the pressure of production deadlines, film budgets and social networks, in the freelancing environment of film and television. The individualism of the industry contrasts with the communities of practice that he experienced while working on publicly funded film projects with young people. He became less inclined to use his skills to perform corporate media work but still feels driven to make films, to 'satisfy this creative urge'. But he no longer has the patience to pretend any longer and to uphold bogus social relations in the hope that they will generate opportunities:

> So for film-makers, it's just a fucking nightmare ... there [are] way, way, way too many film-makers for the amount of jobs there are ... and I'd be better off flipping burgers ... so I suppose in terms of being or having the financial luxury to be a film-maker, well I've come to the end of the line [long pause], but on the other hand, it's fucking good to not have that pressure and stand back from it. And it's nice to know that and, because I am a professional knower of people, that [if] I decided out-and-out to no longer be a film-maker and I was in a bar and there was this guy and I really [couldn't] stand him but normally I'd go say hello 'cause he's the kinda a guy that knows people, and I [would be able to think] nah, I don't have to talk to you today, ya fuckwit. I'm going to have a drink in peace.

The pub is a powerful symbol for the transition that Mike is undergoing. Traditionally a place of after-work drinking, the local was a place of community ties, not of networking and career advancement. It was embedded in the modern division of work and play. So the story of ignoring the gatekeeper represents his release from the need to spend his leisure time grazing for contacts. Why should he have to strike up friendly conversation with someone for whom he had little respect? His words communicate both liberation and defeat. He is no longer forced to walk the freelancer's treadmill but is clearly disappointed at failing to achieve a stellar career. There is much pathos here: he thrives in the creative community of practice, but cannot obtain consistent access to such a community, to reproduce himself as a film-maker in a highly precarious and competitive environment.

Beyond the Social Factory? Priming Creative Renewal

We have argued that many creative aspirants are victims of oversupplied labour markets and stumble before they can even begin to make a living. Policymakers, educators and employers argue that such people have generic and transferable skills that they can bring to other occupations, both inside and outside the creative industries. But this is overly sanguine and ignores the fact that particular skills, including craft skills, will go to waste. And for those who have studied for years to acquire such skills, the suggestion that they reinvent themselves in this way can be deeply dispiriting. Trained actors have the creative skills to sell advertising space, but most do so very reluctantly. As we have seen in this chapter, the decision to set up a business can appear to promise a degree of creative independence such as is not available to those employed by large companies: to conserve their ability to practice the skills they were trained in. But in reality such independence is only available to a privileged few. The great majority of freelancers are condemned to the sweated and precarious margins (e.g. online designers, editors and writers working for micro-payments, competing against a global pool of labour). All of this suggests that creative economic renewal has yet to be achieved, if it is measured by employment and median incomes rather than the wealth of larger creative-industry companies.

So how can this situation be improved? In particular, what new and extended forms of public support, if any, should be available to support creative initiatives? Ironically, as we have seen, the advocates of neo-liberalism have taken up the cause of creativity with gusto. This is in part because the idea of artistic independence has a strange resonance with the ideology of economic individualism. Corporations trade on the oft-expressed sentiment, 'I'm doing what I love and I would do it whether or not I'm paid for it' as a pretext for exploiting workers, and in the quest for innovation, and they seek the labour of those who push cultural boundaries. And although governments in the West spruik the economic importance of culture, the politics of fiscal austerity means that most are engaged in cutting budgets for arts and culture. Those whose ambitions and skills are drawn from private cultural enthusiasms are somehow less deserving of public support.

There is a deep hypocrisy at the heart of this. In the Fordist era, capital accumulation was heavily dependent not just on private finance but on public investment – for example, through worker education/training, transport systems, housing and social infrastructure. However, by comparison, policymakers treat the creative economy as somehow intrinsically self-propelling. While big business can often extract large amounts of public funding to prop up failing enterprises (via 'industry policy'), particularly in areas of high unemployment, small creative entrepreneurs generally have much less leverage. Indeed, for many creative initiatives, the principal form of potential public support is from (usually dwindling and under-resourced) government grant schemes. These are usually one-off, project based and short term. Furthermore, the application, accounting and reporting requirements can be time consuming and onerous, especially for creatives who lack administrative support. A similar predicament is faced by community organizations (including arts bodies), which survive on soft-money, non-recurrent funding sources: the labour and administration often overwhelms their ability to do core work. Moreover, decisions about funding are often guided by the political policy imperatives around urban and regional economic development.

Creatives must often, therefore, seek private finance. Many struggle to persuade banks that their business plans are viable, particularly in fields where global and local competition is intense. In looking at new media, and in particular online gaming development, Pratt, Peake and Ramsden (2000) argue that standard commercial loans do not work for creative industries and argue for a dedicated funding system and new forms of financial aid for cultural production and creative workforces at the micro-enterprise level. Hackett et al. (2000) support the idea of a state-operated 'culture bank' to provide appropriate forms of business support to creative enterprises. Such institutions can both invest in those enterprises/creative projects – with a cut of the profits going back to the public purse – and broker loans from private sources. Additionally, they provide the sort of business support and advice that micro-enterprises generally lack and require. The authors also canvas a variety of other forms of social support for creativity, including the formation of creative local exchange trading schemes, under which skills and expertise can be bartered.

In the absence of such schemes, and with banks reluctant to extend credit, other avenues must be pursued: usually venture capital and philanthropy. Private venture capital is mostly directed at high-risk/high-return digital initiatives, and excludes much of what is done in the creative industries. So many creative freelancers turn to crowdsourcing for money to support their projects, especially in fields like performing arts. This can work for those whose social media networks extend to wealthy people capable of making substantial donations. But, as we saw when considering the search for employment, those who lack appropriate contacts will struggle to raise the resources for their projects. So for all the rhetoric suggesting that creative entrepreneurs will be at the heart of Western economic renewal, the financial system does little to assist them, especially those from socially disadvantaged backgrounds, in implementing their plans.

Conventional social security systems are also poorly suited to meeting the needs of both creative workers/freelancers and others who experience churn and precarity in their working lives. Unemployment benefits schemes are mostly framed around the Fordist wage contract – you are either in work or out of it – but increasing numbers of claimants now require more flexible forms of income support. The process of applying for benefits can be time consuming and frustrating, and require that claimants document their efforts to look for work. For creative workers/freelancers, this depletes the time available for sustaining and reproducing their vocational identities – keeping skills fresh, attending networking events, producing portfolios and so forth – and are effectively a dead weight on the new economy. Some governments – notably in Denmark – have introduced 'flexicurity' arrangements to recognize the volatile working arrangements that prevail in the new economy. But in many places, politicians are sensitive to the popular demonization of benefit recipients, and are reluctant to reform a system based on surveillance, coercion and inflexibility.

In societies where there is not enough work to go around, and where the gap between rich and poor is growing, there is a need to rethink the relationship between work and welfare. Those who advocate a system of Universal Basic Income (UBI) see the state as having the responsibility of providing all residents with enough money to live on, relieving them of some of the pressure to sell their labour in the market (Wright, 2006). UBI[3] can help to redress the growing gulf in power between workers and employers, by giving the former more industrial bargaining strength. It can also help to reverse the long-term decline in real wages and free more people to work in the social economy, undertaking productive activities – for example, care work – for little or no pay. UBI would provide creative aspirants, especially those with little capital behind them, with the ability to continue to practice their skills without the need to be slaves to low-paid day jobs.

The widespread official/technocratic encouragement of workers to develop creative skills – often practised in the spaces outside of formal employment – strengthens the moral case for UBI. Poverty prevents many creative aspirants from practising their creative skills and so the provision of UBI would go some way towards allowing them to do so. As Wright argues (2006, p. 6):

> Engagement in the arts, in politics, and in various kinds of community service would also be facilitated by UBI. Frequently people with serious interests in these kinds of activities would be willing to do them at relatively modest earnings if they were provided through markets – witness the very low standards of living accepted (if reluctantly) by actors, musicians, political activists, and community organizers. The problem for many people is not so much the low earnings, but the inability to find employment in these kinds of activities. UBI makes it possible for people

---

3 We recognise that UBI should not be seen as a replacement for targeted forms of social welfare for those with particular and acute needs (eg sickness, disability and parenting benefits). For many of the recipients of such payments UBI would be insufficient. Furthermore it relies on the operation of a progressive taxation system to make it publicly affordable. UBI should work in conjunction with personal income tax such that the great majority of recipients would be net contributors to state revenues.

to choose to do this kind of activity without having to enter into an employment relation. In this way it contributes to a shift in the balance of power within class relations.

The sort of creative economic renewal that is central to policy requires states to offer more imaginative forms of universal social support appropriate to the situation of post-industrial societies.

The Creative University

As we saw in Chapter 2, there has been a rapid expansion in the numbers of those studying creative courses at school, college and university level. Such institutions provide a carapace for creative endeavours, and most of our interviewees looked back fondly on their time in formal creative education: the teaching and learning, access to equipment and space, the camaraderie of the projects, and the chance for cultural experimentation that is rarely available after graduation. But even public education institutions are now run along corporate lines, with curriculum designed primarily to respond to student demand, with little regard for vocational prospects and outcomes. This means that many students simply fall off a cliff when they graduate. Not only are they left to fend for themselves in highly competitive markets, but they are deprived of the support, mentorship and solidarity they recently enjoyed. This raises the question of whether education institutions should be obliged to provide forms of ongoing support to their graduates.

Some researchers have suggested that universities have the potential to play a larger role in the creative economy. Gilmore and Comunian (2016), for example, discuss their powerful civic role in strengthening local/urban cultural life, intellectual and social capital, in addition to their pedagogical role. They suggest that higher education institutions can play an extended role as creative hubs. In some cases workspaces, facilities and equipment are already in place for existing teaching purposes, and the cost of extending these to support the extramural creative projects, is much lower than building new public infrastructure. Without access to such resources, creative graduates may never be able to develop and capitalize on their creative talents. The university creative hub can rescue them – at least for a period – from being consumed by their day jobs, ending up in occupations that limit their ability to develop new creative ideas. As a condition of access to facilities, administrative and business development support, and the sorts of contacts that institutions can provide, 'creative adjuncts' should have a contractual obligation to return a proportion – perhaps 10 per cent – of the revenues that they generate from their participation in the university hub, including from intellectual property.

Bootstrap Capitalism. Poster from City, University of London 2015

The success of such initiatives requires a level of institutional patience with the projects that occur in these creative spaces. Most will not be commercially successful, but the potential rewards from the few that are may be substantial. The independence that scholars enjoy under the principle of academic freedom should be extended to the larger community involved in the activities of creative hubs. This means that university managers must resist the temptation to try to steer hub projects, refraining from subjecting them to rigid performance indicators (to which their employees are now routinely exposed) and demand for short-term returns. It is worthwhile recognizing lessons from the private sector. Doctorow (2014) describes the unfolding of start-up digital capitalism as a cocktail of chaos and serendipity:

> Startups are weird, intense things. Most of them fail. The ones that succeed usually attain greatness by abandoning everything they set out to do and figuring out something altogether new that was only revealed through the disastrous failure of the original idea. They are fizzy. They draw in people – often very talented people – and spit them out again. A common pattern in startups is to go to work for one, watch it implode and team up with a colleague or two to move on to another startup; repeat several times. [...] Startups are a product of a critical mass of startup-ey people who [...] trial-and-error their way through several improbable ideas on their way to discovering unsuspected new opportunities that occasionally pay off in mind-boggling ways.

This suggests that experiments, happenstance and multi-disciplinary collaboration – including a co-presence of artists and those with entrepreneurial skills – propel innovation. Free play is central to creative innovation and – outside the velvet womb of Silicon Valley – rarely available to those working under corporate constraint.

The university's creative hub links can operate at an institutional as well as an individual level. Some universities have been very successful in cultivating the 'science park' model of corporate collaboration: techno-burbs springing up alongside and in symbiotic connection with campuses, companies and STEM scholars working together. Many also now have incubators that house small digital start-ups, although, despite being labelled as creative, such start-ups are often quite conventional businesses.[4] By contrast, universities have been less effective in working with artistis and arts/cultural organizations in much of the world. Cantor (2005) observes that in the United States universities have long provided creative people with performing-arts opportunities and although they work with arts bodies, neither have articulated this relationship or taken full advantage of it (Cantor 2005, p. 2). Such collaborations can involve the university in urban creative regeneration, especially those located in areas where land values have not been rapidly inflated by the gentrification spiral. By investing in spaces outside their boundaries they can also potentially provide the local public with cultural benefits (Cantor 2005, p. 18).

The neo-liberal view of universities depicts them as competitors in the education marketplace with no long-term obligation to their student-customers. To fulfil their mission they must provide quality education and confer credentials on those who meet the requisite standards. They provide no guarantee on the future value of those credentials in the labour market (as one university manager was heard to remark, 'it's like … we can sell you a car but we can't guarantee you'll be able to drive it in Monaco'). However, a higher ethical standard applies in public education than neo-liberalism would suggest. The idea of an enduring obligation to alumni is based on a widespread public acknowledgment that, as employment opportunities decline, so does the utility of credentials, even those that might once have been gold plated. Many diplomas and degrees provide very little labour market leverage and, as we

---

4 In recent years some universities have established 'makerspaces' for artists and craftworkers, and fabrication laboratories – of 'fablabs' – that accommodate high-tech manufacturing, especially with the use of digital printers. However, this is relatively underdeveloped and very few of those who graduate in fields like design have will have the opportunity to participate in such spaces.

have argued, training is going to waste as graduates end up in jobs that are not worthy of their skills.

Policymakers have long declared that creativity will spawn economic renewal but unless there is extended public support for creative trainees/aspirants, then such declarations will ring hollow, especially in the ears of graduates who are strangled by student debt. Education institutions can provide such support efficiently, and should be funded to do so. They are appropriate places in which to supply creative alumni with ongoing training, networking opportunities and access to infrastructure/equipment. They can also serve as a point of anchorage for the creative-professional-identity claims of struggling graduates. However, in order to achieve such reforms and the funding required to support them, there is a need for a larger debate that recognizes the changing nature of work and breaks with the market view of post-school education.

Conclusion

A central tenet of neoclassical economics is that the market provides the most efficient means to allocate scarce resources and generate individual and collective prosperity. But in the supply and demand for creative labour we can see a textbook example of market failure. The number of trained creative aspirants vastly exceeds the ability of the labour market to make efficient use of their skills. Although employers, both in creative industries and beyond, often claim that they give their workers scope to express these skills, this usually means that they are dressing up mundane labour to be something more than it is. And despite the ideology of feral enterprise suggesting that creative aspirants can prosper as freelancers and also retain their creative autonomy, many find themselves caught in a poverty trap, chasing small commissions, projects and grants, and with hardly any time and opportunity to apply their skills to genuinely creative work. The 'social factory' is little more than the quintessential form of new capitalism: of hypercompetition, the individualization of risk, and far from encouraging the flourishing of the commons, it actually undermines social cooperation. Economists argue that in response to this situation the 'economically rational' individual will refrain from investing time and energy to train for a creative career and instead aim for something more viable. Yet, encouraged to 'go for their dreams', young people continue to train in fields like film, performing arts, design and music in vast numbers. Education institutions – both public and private – continue to stoke this demand with little regard for the fate of their graduates. As we have seen, most of those who come from socially disadvantaged backgrounds find it difficult to maintain their creative identities as they face the prospect of precarity and low pay. Even middle-class aspirants like Stuart can find themselves consigned to the low-paid and unfulfilling margins. We have argued in this chapter that governments have a moral obligation to support creative aspirants beyond the point at which their formal training ends, and that this should take the form of resourcing post-school education institutions as creative hubs – places that encourage the formation of communities of practice, creative projects and, importantly, provide business and administrative support, allowing creative projects to realize any commercial potential. The case for this ongoing resourcing of creativity is perhaps sometimes difficult to see. This is because creativity lies at the junction of the private and public, and is associated with leisure rather than work. It is easy to take the view that even those who are professionally trained in creative skills are just having fun and that if they cannot make a living from it, they are not deserving of much social support. The Australian minister for education recently referred to creative graduates as having made 'lifestyle choices' (Birmingham, 2016). However, if, as a society, we encourage young people to undertake creative training, the cost of which, to some extent at least, they have to bear individually, and if their qualifications provide very little labour-market leverage, then there exists a moral obligation on governments to provide at least some ongoing social support to them after graduation. In an era of declining employment opportunities for young people in the West, the case for the creative university is clear.

CONCLUSION: DON'T CALL US, WE'LL CALL YOU

The climactic point in the reality/talent television show comes when the competitors are summoned before the judging panel. The formula is the same whether they have sung, danced, walked the catwalk or tried to cook the perfect gourmet dish. After the performance there is a moment of contrived intensity – a dramatic pause, a drum roll, the spectacle of the eager competitor on tenterhooks. On the judging panel we usually find an assortment of old stagers – performers, talent agents, producers and so forth – and a vaudevillian mixture of the kind and the cruel. On the one side are the 'hiss-the-villain' figures like Simon Cowell, whose role is to ridicule the nervous, inept or faltering performances. On the other are the more kindly judges, who are there to soften the blow of rejection with maternal or avuncular condolences and encouragement. As the losers slink off in crestfallen bewilderment – don't call us, we'll call you – we, the viewers, can experience that moment of schadenfreude, of voyeuristic pleasure that comes from others' misfortune, especially those whose talent does not quite match their confidence. Who, after all, has not had their bubble burst by critics at some stage? The winners are left to dance a euphoric jig. But their prize might only be the chance to endure yet another round of critical scrutiny. Like online/video games, the more levels you conquer, the more it becomes double or quits.

It is easy to be scornful of this process, of its cheap and superficial slickness, of the do-or-die pressure, the foolish vulnerability of the competitors, the formulaic commercialism. Why would you parade your talents in front of these smug and self-important gatekeepers? Why expose your art to the blowtorch of commercial television? But this misses the ideological point. The reality television spectacle is a powerful allegory of the postmodern career, which we all, by now, recognize as both compelling and perilous. It is the very antithesis of the modern career, characterized by the slow accretion of skill, credentials, peer esteem, and loyalty to a profession, craft and community. In the modern career, the future was stable and predictable; opportunities would open to those with talent. By contrast, the postmodern career narrative suggests that life is defined by key moments, often serendipitous and unforeseeable, at which we must show ourselves to be worthy. In these circumstances, there is no normal selection process – advertisement, application, merit-based assessment – and you cannot rely on formal industrial rights, gender equity or equal opportunity policies to protect you. Talent is a necessary but not sufficient condition for postmodern career progression and plenty of very gifted people receive scant reward and recognition. In creative fields, where most work is allocated informally, aspirants must accept that powerful people are able to make snap, capricious evaluations of their work. The gatekeepers are inscrutable and unaccountable: there is no avenue through which to appeal their decisions.

Such eviscerating judgements contrast starkly with the creative encouragements of youth.

In this book we have charted the ways in which creativity has changed meaning. A word that once referred primarily to the cultural freewheeling that took place outside of work has become synonymous with entrepreneurial innovation. Capitalism's conscription of creativity has also subtly changed the idea of youth and youth culture. Fifty years ago, those shepherding people through adolescence would most likely have viewed youth culture as so much rubble littering the path to adulthood. Young people might be drawn into subcultural practice or artistic introspection, but this was only a temporary bewitchment, and would eventually be abandoned for a steady working life in an office or factory. Now the idea of creative economic renewal suggests to youth that the symbolic creativity that was concerned with avoiding or resisting the strictures of the parent culture – deferring the transition to adulthood – becomes the raw material for building a calling, a public identity and then a career.

The pedagogical, parental and official encouragement of creative skills has led many youth who in an earlier era might have left school early to enter the workforce to enrol in post-school creative training courses. But most of them graduate into highly competitive creative-labour markets that rarely operate by the meritocratic principles that apply in education. Aspirants who lack cultural, social and economic resources will find few lucrative outlets for their skills. They are handicapped both by their remoteness from the creative clusters that operate in expensive global cities and because they lack the cultural capital and network contacts that open doors. So, in the face of meagre incomes and precarious employment, many are forced into periods of extended dependence on parents, who themselves are bewildered by the new world of work, and who might well suspect that their child has been led down a blind alley. Creativity has thus become part of the story of elongated transition from youth to adulthood in late modernity.

We began this book with this quote from an online job advertisement – 'Are you passionate about pet accessories?' – to illustrate the designs that new capitalism has on workers. It is not enough for them to give time and labour; they must also surrender their souls. In the creative economy, workers can have no secrets. There is no emotion or affect, nothing from the private or intimate realms that cannot be brought to the workplace, as Ariel Hochschild (2003) argued. Our research demonstrates that people are forced to put their creativity to work in unanticipated ways, primarily in the cause of selling things, and that, in these circumstances, *the idea of creativity* can lose much of its inheritance: romantic, bohemian and subcultural. But creative workers rarely abandon such associations without a fight.

The notion of the creative economy is not only about stretching the word so as to allow capital to colonize symbolic expression. It is also about disciplining labour:

> My father had a steady, predictable career which carried him through to a well earned, properly funded and enjoyable retirement. ... I am not yet forty, I have already had several mini-careers ... I am one of Charles Handy's portfolio workers ... I live on my wits. (Leadbeater, 1999, p. 1)

Since Charles Leadbeater wrote this about the new shape of working life in his book *Living on Thin Air*, creativity has become a central device to turn workers from obedient Fordist 'hands' to just-in-time workers: transferable, entrepreneurial and individualistic. To survive, they must become new capitalism's court jesters: slaves to the market's fickle rhythms, jumping eagerly towards the serendipitous opportunity that it throws up, forging a disposition of frenetic readiness. Workers must mirror capital's perturbation, and dance to its whims and impulses. In the risk society (Beck, 1992), we must habituate ourselves to the idea of perpetual disruption caused by global competition, digital communication and rapid stylistic innovation. In these circumstances, flexibility becomes a moral imperative. Nothing stays in place very long, and so the new worker must not rest easy, and must dispense with long-term planning in favour of tactical opportunism.

The struggle over creativity is both semantic and material. It is tied to the project of refashioning labour for new times, but as our interviewees have shown, labour is not as plastic as capital would like. The residual habits, values and impulses are a brake on the new economy. Creative aspirants, especially those from working-class backgrounds, rarely assimilate instantly or easily to this demand for flexibility, and to the commercialized or embedded idea of their vocation. If they do so – and, unlike Leadbeater (1999), many do not – it is by increments and usually with regret at the loss of creativity's youthful ludic roots. We have shown that in the typical 'creative biography', aspirants from poorer backgrounds regularly confront a series of transactions – points of thorny reckoning – where they are forced to barter their skills in response to financial and social pressures and diminishing vocational options for meaningful symbolic expression. Poverty and precarity force certain compromises: around how to manage the low-paid day job and still find time to do creative work and build the creative career; whether to set yourself up as a small entrepreneur when no job offers come along; whether to apply for the corporate job with better money but little fulfilment; whether to retrain in a field where the prospects are more solid.

We have argued that the promise of creative capitalism remains largely unfulfilled; that it is a fantasy of regeneration. It is one thing to recognize the ludic and iconoclastic sources of insurgent capitalism but it is another to find and harness those sources. The grey-suited technocrats who crave the great leap forward and the bounty of intellectual property are incapable of generating that bounty on their own. In the ruins of scientific management, the onus has shifted to the workers. Jobs that are advertised as creative often turn out to be old, routinized work dressed up as new. This is a central paradox of the new economy: employers are dissatisfied with the skills of their workers and the workers feel their jobs don't make best use of their skills (Haukka, 2011). There is a shared disappointment on each side of the employment contract.

Except that most workers are not employees, but freelancers in the gig economy, victims of the drive to outsource risk. Or they are temporary and disposable employees – short term, project based or interns – to whom no long-term commitment is made. So in this climate of thin prospects, many remain in the liminal zone between amateurism and professionalism. Keeping your creative identity alive involves more than just an act of will, it requires you to engage in the ancillary work of professional reproduction: of networking, updating skills, promoting your business. This is difficult for those who lack the resources to bear the long periods with little or no income. It is not just financial pressures but the 'fear of falling' – the anxiety that appears to come with coming from a poor background – that forces their hand.

We can see the call to creativity as part of the larger ideology of neo-liberalism, of individual choice/sovereignty and the idea of the pursuit of a calling. Ironically, at a time in history when futures are more opaque, outcomes more uncertain, skills and jobs more transient, the rhetoric of questing heroic individualism is more hysterical. Young people hear the message that '*you can be anything you want to be*'. It is a moral duty to avoid sleepwalking through life: '*Shoot for the stars*' and '*don't die wondering.*' This reflexive element of late modernity has been thoroughly raked over by social scientists. However, our work shows that far from embracing these calls unconditionally, there are residual impulses that frame and delimit the way young people approach working life. These values based on the virtue of communities of practice, of mentorship, loyalty and craft, and the right to protection from alienated labour, generate resistance to the flighty, project-based individualism that increasingly characterizes working life. As E. P. Thompson suggested in *The Making of the English Working Class* (1963), social class is an historical trajectory, a formation that is lived over time. So while modes of production can change rapidly, workers rarely do. The collective cultures of labour have inertia.

So for many aspirants the creative career is characterized by gradual disillusionment, the pressure of poverty, dissimulation of creative skills and work that does not utilize their skills. This represents a form of social betrayal and raises a troubling ethical question: What sort of society encourages gifted people to climb and strive, to perfect their craft, to express their creative talents, when there is nothing for them at the pinnacle of achievement but a treadmill of mundane work and poverty? If governments are not prepared to invest resources to support creative aspirants to overcome their precarious circumstances – by continuing to educate them and give them access to creative spaces and equipment, and by providing better forms of income support – then the public dream of creative economic renewal will be stillborn and a generation of young people will have their working lives blighted by curdling resentment.

BIBLIOGRAPHY

Abercrombie, N., Hill, S & Turner, B.S. (1986). *Sovereign individuals of capitalism*. Crows Nest: Allen and Unwin.

Abrams, F. (2009). High school delusional. *New Statesman* 1 October, http://www.newstatesman.com/society/2009/10/labour-market-young-wilson accessed 2 February 2014.

Adkins, L. (1999) Community and economy: a retraditionalization of gender? *Theory, Culture & Society*, 16(1): 199–239.

Alonso, L. E. & Martinez, M. L. (eds) (2006). *Employment relations in a changing society: assessing the post-Fordist paradigm*. Basingstoke: Palgrave Macmillan.

Australian Bureau of Statistics (ABS) (2013). ABS census, IBIS world industry reports, SGS economics and planning.

ABS (2013). Australian film industry employment (cat. no. 8679.0).

ABS (2009). Job flexibility of casual employees (cat. no. 6105.0).

ABS (2014). Labour force Australia July (cat. no. 6202.0).

ABS (2015). Labour force Australia (cat. no. 6202.0).

ABS (2014). Youth unemployment figures (cat. no. 6202.0).

Allen, K. & Hollingworth, S. (2013). 'Sticky subjects' or 'cosmopolitan creatives'? Social class, place and urban young people's aspirations for work in the knowledge economy, *Urban Studies*, 50(3): 499–517.

Anthias, F. (2004) Social stratification and social inequality: models of intersectionality and identity, in Devine, F., Savage, M., Scott, J. & Crompton, R. (eds), *Rethinking class: culture, identity & lifestyle*. Houndsmill, Basingstoke, Hampshire: Palgrave Macmillan

Arts Council of England (2015). Contribution of the arts and culture industry to the national economy. http://www.artscouncil.org.uk/sites/default/files/download-file/Arts_culture_contribution_to_economy_report_July_2015.pdf.

Bakhshi, H., Freeman, A., & Higgs, P. L. (2012). *A dynamic mapping of the UK's creative industries*. (2013). http://www.nesta.org.uk/sites/default/files/a_dynamic_mapping_of_the_creative_industries.pdf, accessed 17 November 2017.

Banks, M. (2010). Craft labour and creative industries. *International Journal of Cultural Policy*, 13: 305–21.

Banks, M. & Milestone, K. (2011). *Individualization, gender and cultural work*. Oxford: Blackwell Publishers.

Barton, G. (2016). *Don't get a job, make a job: how to make it as a creative graduate*. London: Lawrence King.

BBC News (2011, March 10). London's tech city growth hailed by PM Cameron. http://www.bbc.com/news/technology-15671829 (accessed October 10, 2017).

Beck, U., Giddens, A. & Lash, S. (1994). *Reflexive modernization: politics, tradition and aesthetics in the modern social order*. California, Stanford: Stanford University Press

Beck, U. (1992). *Risk society: towards a new modernity*. London, Thousand Oaks, New Delhi: Sage Publications.

Beck, U. (2000). *The brave new world of work*. Cambridge, MA: Polity.

Beck, U. & Beck-Gernsheim, E. (2002). *Individualization: institutionalized individualism and its social and political consequences*. London: Thousand Oaks; New Delhi: Sage Publications.

Becker, H. (1982). *Art worlds*. Berkeley, Los Angeles, London: University of California Press.

Bennett, A. & Hodkinson, P. (2012). Introduction, in *Ageing and youth cultures: music, style and identity*, Bennett, A. & Hodkinson, P. (eds), London, New York: Berg.

Bennett, D. (2009). Academy and the real world: developing realistic notions of career in the performing arts. Arts and Humanities in Higher Education, 8(3): 309-327

Bird, M. (2015). Italy's youth unemployment just reached a new record high,. *Business Insider Australia*, 1 August, http://www.businessinsider.com.au/italys-youth-unemployment-just-hit-a-new-record-high-heres-whats-going-wrong-2015-7?r=UK&IR=T, accessed 12 October 2016.

Blair, H. (2001). You're only as good as your last job: the labour process and labour market in the British film industry. *Work, Employment & Society*, 15(1): 149-169

Blair, H. (2003). Winning and losing in flexible labour markets: the formation and operation of networks and interdependence in the UK film industry. *Sociology*, 37(4): 677-694

Blair, H. (2009). Active Networking: action, social structure and the process of networking, in Mckinlay, A., and Smith, C. (eds) *Creative Labour: working in the creative industries*. Houndsmill, Bassingstoke, Hampshire: Palgrave Macmillan

Blanchflower, D. (2015). Britain's hidden army of underemployed,. *The Independent*, 29 April, http://www.independent.co.uk/news/business/analysis-and-features/our-hidden-army-of-under-employed-10211368.html, accessed 25 October 2017

Boltanski, L. & Chiapello, E. (2006). *The new spirit of capitalism*. Trans. G. Elliott, London: Verso.

Bourdieu, P. (1971). Intellectual field and creative project, in M.F.D. Young (ed.), *Knowledge and control: new directions for the sociology of education*, London: Collier-Macmillan.

Bourdieu, P. (1984). *Distinction: a social critique of the judgement of taste*. Cambridge, MA: Harvard University Press.

Bourgois, P. (1995). *In search of respect: selling crack in the El Barrio*. Cambridge: Cambridge University Press.

Braverman, H. (1974). *Labor and monopoly capital: the degradation of work in the twentieth century*. New York, London: Monthly Review Press.

Brophy, E. (2011). Language put to work: cognitive capitalism, call centre labour, and worker inquiry, *Journal of Communication Inquiry*, 35(4): 411–17.

Brotherhood of St Laurence (2014). Young and underemployed in Australia, Melbourne.

Birmingham, S. (2016). New VET student loans course list focussed on employment outcomes, http://www.senatorbirmingham.com.au/Latest-News/ID/3238/New-VET-Student-Loans-course-list-focussed-on-employment-outcomes, accessed 19 February 2017.

Bounds, A. (2015). Small business growth returns to pre-recession levels says study., *Financial Times*, 15 June, https://www.ft.com/content/c0bbf34c-1335-11e5-bd3c-00144feabdc0

Burgess, J., Campbell, I. & May, R. (2008). Pathways from casual employment to economic security: the Australian experience, *Social Indicators Research*, 88: 161–78.

Burtch, G., Carnahan, S. & Greenwood, B. N. (2016). Can You Gig it? An Empirical Examination of the Gig Economy and Entrepreneurial Activity, *Working Paper No. 1308*,

March 2016 http://questromworld.bu.edu/platformstrategy/files/2016/06/platform2016_paper_1.pdf

Campbell, I. (2004). Casual work and casualisation: how does Australia compare?, *Labour and Industry,* 15(2): 85–111.

Campbell, I. (2001). Casual employees and the training deficit: exploring employer calculations and choices, *International Journal of Employment Studies,* 9(1): 61–101.

Campbell, I. (2010). The rise in precarious employment and union responses in Australia, in C. Thornley, S. Jefferys and B. Appay (eds), *Globalization and precarious forms of production and employment: challenges for workers and union.* London: Edward Elgar.

Campbell, I., Whitehouse, G. & Baxter, J. (2009). Australia: casual employment, part-time employment and the resilience of the male breadwinner model, in L. Vosko, M. MacDonald & I. Campbell (eds), *Gender and the contours of precarious employment.* London: Routledge.

Campbell, I. (2013). An historical perspective on insecure work in Australia, *The Queensland Journal of Labour History,* 16: 6–24.

Cantor, N. (2005). Collaborations on the Creative 'Campus', Office of the Chancellor, Paper 20

Caves, R. E. (2000). *Creative industries: contracts between art and commerce.* Cambridge, MA: Harvard University Press.

Chan, S. & Tweedie, D. (2015). Precarious work and reproductive Insecurity, *Social Alternatives,* 34:4–13.

Creative Industries Innovation Centre (CIIC) (2013). *Valuing Australia's creative industries.* Brisbane, Canberra, Hobart, Melbourne, Sydney: SGS Economics and Planning Pty Ltd.

City of Sydney (2016). Creative and digital, http://www.cityofsydney.nsw.gov.au/business/business-support/business-in-your-sector/key-industries/creative-and-digital

Clark, D. (2009). Crunching creativity: an attempt to measure creative employment, *Creative Industries Journal,* 2(3): 217–30.

Clarke, J. (1976). The skinheads and the magical recovery of community, in S. Hall & T. Jefferson (eds), *Resistance through rituals: youth subcultures in postwar Britain.* London: Hutchinson.

Clare, M. & Johnson, R. (1986). Unpublished Paper.

Clarke, J. & Critcher, C. (1985). *The devil makes work: leisure in capitalist Britain.* London: Macmillan.

CM Council (2007). http://mcm.arts.gov.au/sites/default/files/building-a-creative-innovation-economy.pdf, accessed 25 August 2016.

Cohen, P. (1972). Sub-cultural conflict and working class community, *Working Papers in Cultural Studies,* No.2, Birmingham: University of Birmingham.

Cohen, P. (1999). Apprenticeship a la mode? Some reflections on learning as cultural labour, in P. Ainley & H. Rainbird (eds), *Apprenticeship: towards a new paradigm of learning.* London: Kogan Page.

Connell, R. W. (1995). *Masculinities.* St Leonards: Allen & Unwin.

Connell, R. W. (2003). Working-class families and the new secondary education, *Australian Journal of Education,* 47(3): 237–52.

Creative Australia. (2013). *National cultural policy.,* http://creative australia.arts.gov.au/full-policy

Creative Industries Innovation Centre (CIIC) (2013). *Valuing Australia's creative industries: final report.* CIIC, Brisbane, Canberra, Hobart, Melbourne, Sydney: SGS Economics and Planning.

Creative Industries Task Force (CITF) (2001). Creative industries mapping document., http://www.culture.gov.au.uk/creative/mapping.html

Christopherson, S. (2008). Beyond the self-expressive creative worker: an industry perspective on entertainment media, *Theory, Culture & Society*, 25(7-8): 73-95

Crofts, J., Cuervo, H., Wyn, J., Smith, G. & Woodman, D. (2015). Life patterns: ten years following Generation Y. Melbourne: Melbourne Graduate School of Education.

Cunningham, S. (2013). *Hidden innovation: policy, industry and the creative sector*. St Lucia: University of Queensland Press.

Davis, J. R. (2012). Punk, ageing and the expectations of adult life, in *Ageing and youth cultures: music, style and identity*, Bennett, A. & Hodkinson, P. (eds), London, New York: Berg.

De Bono, E. (2015). *Serious creativity: how to be creative under pressure and turn ideas into action*. New York: Random House.

De Peuter, G. (2001). Creative economy and labor precarity: a contested convergence, *Journal of Communication Inquiry*, 35(4): 417–25.

Department of Culture, Media and Sport (DCMS) (1998). Creative industries mapping document. London: DCMS.

Department of Culture, Media and Sport (DCMS) (2015). Creative industries: focus on employment., https://www.gov.uk/government/uploads/system/uploads/attachment_data/file/439714/Annex_C_-_Creative_Industries_Focus_on_Employment_2015.pdf

De Stefano, V. (2015). The rise of the 'just-in-time workforce': on-demand work, crowd work and labour protection in the 'gig-economy', *Comparative Labor Law & Policy Journal*, Forthcoming; Bocconi Legal Studies Research Paper No. 2682602. Available at SSRN: https://ssrn.com/abstract=2682602 or http://dx.doi.org/10.2139/ssrn.2682602.

DiMaggio, P. (1977). Market structure, the creative process, and popular culture: toward an organizational reinterpretation of mass-culture theory, *Journal of Popular Culture*, 11(2): 436–52.

Doctorow, C. (2014). The slow death of Silicon Roundabout., *The Guardian*, 10 March, https://www.theguardian.com/cities/2014/mar/10/slow-death-of-silicon-roundabout

Dwyer, P. & Wyn, J. (2001). *Youth, education and risk*. London: Routledge Falmer.

Ehrenreich, B. (1989). *Fear of falling: the inner life of the middle class*. New York: Pantheon Books.

Ekinsmyth, C. (2013). Managing the business of everyday life: the roles of space and place in 'mumpreneurship', *International Journal of Entrepreneurial Behaviour & Research*, 19(5): 525–46.

Evans, K. (2007). Concepts of bounded agency in education, work, and the personal lives of young adults, *International Journal of Psychology*, 42(2): 85–93.

Florida, R. (2003). *The rise of the creative class*. New York: Basic.

Friedman, G. (2014). Workers without employers: shadow corporations and the rise of the gig economy, *Review of Keynesian Economics*, 2(2) Summer 2014: 171–88.

Furlong, A. & Cartmel, F. (1997). *Young people and social change*. Philadelphia: Open University Press.

Garnham, N. (2005). From cultural to creative industries: an analysis of the implications of the 'creative industries' approach to arts and media policy making in the United Kingdom, *International Journal of Cultural Policy*, 11, 15–29.

Gagnier, R. (1991). *Subjectivities: a history of self-representation in Britain 1832–1920*. Oxford: Oxford University Press.

Geertz, C. (1993). *The interpretation of cultures*. London: Fontana.

Giddens, A. (1991). *Modernity and self-identity: self and society in the late modern age.* Cambridge: Polity.

Gill, R. (2002). Cool, creative and egalitarian? Exploring gender in project-based new media in Euro, *Information, Communication and Society,* 5: 70–89.

Gill, R. (2008). Culture and subjectivity in neoliberal and postfeminist times, *Subjectivity,* 25: 432–55.

Gill, R. (2009). Creative biographies in new media: social innovation in web work, in A. Pratt & P. Jeffcutt (eds), *Creativity, innovation and the cultural economy.* London, New York: Routledge.

Gill, R. & Pratt, A. (2008). In the social factory?: Immaterial labour, precariousness and cultural work, *Theory, Culture & Society,* 25 (7–8): 1–30.

Gill, R. (2010). Life is a pitch: managing the self in new media work, in M. Deuze (ed.), *Managing media work.* London, Thousand Oaks, New Delhi: Sage Publications.

Gilmore. A. & Comunian, R. (2016). Beyond the campus: higher education, cultural policy and the creative economy, *International Journal of Cultural Policy,* 22(1): 1–9.

Giroux, H. (1983). *Theory and resistance in education: a pedagogy for the opposition.* Amherst: Bergin and Garvey.

Giroux, H. (1999). Rething cultural politics and radical pedagogy in the work of Antonio Gramsci, *Educational Theory,* 49(1): 1–9

Gitell, R. V. & Vidal, A. (1998). *Community organizing: building social capital as a development strategy.* Newbury Park: Sage Publications.

Goffman, E. (1959). *The presentation of self in everyday life.* Garden City, New York: Doubleday.

Gorz, A. (1989). *The traitor.* London, New York: Verso.

Graeber, D. (2013). On the phenomenon of bullshit jobs., *Strike! Magazine,* 17 August 2013.

Gregg, M. (2011). *Work's Intimacy.* Cambridge: Polity Press

Gulli, B. (2005). *Labor of fire: the ontology of labour between economy and culture.* Philadelphia: Temple University Press.

Hackett, K., Ramsden, P., Sattar, D. & Guene, C. (2000). *Banking on Culture: new financial instruments for expanding the cultural sector in Europe.* London: North West Arts Board.

Hall, S. (1980). Encoding/decoding, in S. Hall., D. Hobson, A. Lowe & P. Willis (eds), *Culture, media, language: working papers in cultural studies,* 1972–79, 128–38, London: Hutchinson.

Hardt, M & Negri, A. (2009). *Commonwealth,* Cambridge: Harvard University Press

Harney, S. (2010). Creative industries debate: unfinished business: labour, management and the creative industries, *Cultural Studies,* 24/3: 431–44.

Haylett, C. (2001). Illegitimate subjects? Abject whites, neoliberal modernization and middle class multiculturalism, *Environment and Planning A,* 19: 351–70.

Haukka, S. (2011). Education to work transitions of aspiring creatives, *Cultural Trends,* 20: 41–64.

Heckman, J. J. & LaFontaine, P. A. (2010). The American high school graduation rate: trends and patterns, *Review of Economic Statistics,* May, 92(2): 244–62.

Hebdige, D. (1979). *Subculture: the meaning of style.* London: Methuen & Co. Ltd.

Hesmondhalgh, D. (2007). *The cultural industries.* London, Thousand Oaks, New Delhi, Singapore: Sage Publications.

Hesmondhalgh, D. & Baker, S. (2011). *Creative labour: media work in three cultural industries.* London, New York: Routledge.

Hesmondhalgh, D. & Percival, N. (2014). Unpaid work in the UK television and film industries: resistance and changing attitudes, *European Journal of Communication,* 29(2): 188–203.

Ho, C. & Alcorso, C. (2004). Migrants and employment: challenging the success story, *Journal of Sociology*, 40(3): 237–59.

Hochschild, A. R. (2003). *The managed heart: commercialization of human feeling*. Berkeley: University of California Press.

Hollands, R. (1990). *The long transition: class, culture and youth training*. London: Macmillan Education.

Huntley, R. (2006). *The world according to Y: inside the new adult generation*. Crows Nest: Allen & Unwin.

I-Want-In, http://www.industry.nsw.gov.au/__data/assets/pdf_file/0004/56299/I-WANT-IN.pdf, accessed 25 August 2016.

Idriss, S. (2018). *Young migrant identities: creativity and masculinity*. London: Routledge.

Institute of Family Studies (2013). CFCA Paper, No.16 – July 2013.

Ingeldew, J. (2016). *How to have great ideas: a guide to creative thinking*. London: Laurence King.

Judkins, R. (2016). *The art of creative thinking: 89 ways to see things differently*. London: Penguin.

Kelly, P. & Kenway, J. (2001). Managing youth transitions in the network society, *British Journal of Sociology of Education*, 22(1): 19–33.

Kenway, J., Kraack, A. & Hickey-Moody, A. (2006). *Masculinity beyond the metropolis*. Basingstoke: Palgrave-Macmillan

Kierkegaard, S. *Journalen JJ*:167 (1843), *Søren Kierkegaards Skrifter*, Søren Kierkegaard Research Center, Copenhagen, 1997 volume 18

Kuhn, A. (2000). A journey through memory, in S. Radstone (ed.), *Memory and methodology*. Oxford: Berg.

Lacey, S. (2013). You can go it alone and design yourself a future., *Sydney Morning Herald*, 23–24 March , p. 14.

Landry, C. (2000). *The creative city*. London: Taylor and Francis

Lash, S. (1994). Reflexivity and its doubles: structure, aesthetics, community, in U. Beck, A. Giddens & S. Lash, (eds), Reflexive Modernization: Politics, Tradition and Aesthetic, 110–73.

Lave, J. & Wenger, E. (1991). *Situated learning: legitimate peripheral participation*. Cambridge: Cambridge University Press.

Lazzarato, M. (1996). Immaterial labour, in M. Hardt & P. Virno (eds), *Radical thought in Italy: a potential politics*. Minneapolis: University of Minnesota Press.

Leadbeater, C. (1999). *Living on thin air: the new economy*. London: Viking.

Lloyd, R. (2006). *Neo-bohemia: art and commerce in the postindustrial city*. New York: Routledge.

Luckman, S. (2015). *Craft and the creative economy*. London: Palgrave Macmillan.

Luckman, S. (2016). Micro-enterprise as work-life 'Magical Solution', in L. Adkins & S. Dever (eds), *The post-Fordist sexual contract: working and living in contingency*. London: Palgrave Macmillan, 91–108.

McCarthy, T. (2016). The best, if worst paid, job I ever had., *The New Yorker*, 10 October, http://www.newyorker.com/magazine/2016/10/10/the-best-if-worst-paid-job-i-ever-had

McDowell, L. (2000). Learning to serve? Employment aspirations and attitutes of young working-class men in an era of labour market restructuring, *Gender, Place and Culture*, 7 (4): 389-416

McRobbie, A. (2002). Fashion culture: creative work, female individualization, *Feminist Review*, 71(1): 52–62.

McRobbie, A. (2002a). From Holloway to Hollywood: happiness at work in the new cultural economy, in P. duGay & M. Pryke (eds), *Cultural economy: cultural analysis and commercial life*. London, Thousand Oaks, New Delhi: Sage Publications.

McRobbie, A. (2002b). Clubs to companies: notes on the decline of political culture in speeded up creative worlds, *Cultural Studies*, 16: 516–31.

McWilliams, D. (2015). *The flat white economy*. London: Gerald Duckworth.

Maffesoli, M. (1995). *The time of the tribes: The decline of individualism in mass society*. Thousand Oaks, California: Sage Publications.

Marazzi, C. (2008). *Capital and language: from the new economy to the war economy*. Los Angeles: Semiotext(e).

Morgan, G. & Nelligan, P. (2014). Labile labour: gender, flexibility and creative work, *Sociological Review*, 63: 66–83.

Murnane, R. J. (2013). U.S. high school graduation rates: patterns and explanations, *Journal of Economic Literature*, 51(2): 370–422.

Murgia, A. (2015). Obverse and reverse sides of precariousness: young highly educated workers between passions and skill mismatch, *Social Alternatives*, 34(4): 14–21.

National Cultural Policy discussion paper (2011). http://www.australiantheatreforum.com.au/wp-content/uploads/2014/05/national-cultural-policy-discussion-paper.pdf

Nayak, A. (2003). 'Ivory lives': economic restructuring and the making of whiteness in a post-industrial youth community, *European Journal of Cultural Studies* 2003, 6(3): 305–25.

Nayak, A. (2003). *Race, place and globalization: youth cultures in a changing world*. Oxford: Berg.

Nayak, A. (2006). Displaced masculinities: chavs, youth and class in the post-industrial city, *Sociology*, 40/5: 813–31.

Neilson, B. & Rossiter, N. (2008). Precarity as a political concept, or, Fordism as exception, *Theory, Culture & Society*, 25(7–8): 51–72.

Negri, A. (1989). *The politics of subversion: a manifesto for the twenty-first century*. Cambridge: Polity.

Nixon, D. (2006). 'I just like working with my hands': employment aspirations and the meaning of work for low-skilled unemployed men in Britain's service economy, *Journal of Education and Work*, 19(2): 201–17.

Nixon, (2009). 'I can't put a smiley face on': working-class masculinity, emotional labour and service work in the 'new economy', *Gender, Work and Organisation*, 16(3): 300–22.

Oakely, K. (2006). Include us out – economic development and social policy in the creative industries, *Cultural Trends*, 15: 255–73.

OECD.org (2012). https://www.oecd.org/edu/EAG%202012_e-book_EN_200912.pdf

Office for the Arts (2011). National Cultural Policy: Discussion Paper, Department of Prime Minister and Cabinet, Canberra.

Office of National Statistics (2015). Contracts with No Guaranteed Hours: 2015, https://www.ons.gov.uk/employmentandlabourmarket/peopleinwork/earningsandworkinghours/articles/contractswithnoguaranteedhours/2015-09-02, accessed 2 September 2016.

Osborne, H. (2016). Uber loses right to classify UK drivers as self-employed., *The Guardian*, 28 October, https://www.theguardian.com/technology/2016/oct/28/uber-uk-tribunal-self-employed-status

Perlin, R. (2011). *Intern nation: how to earn nothing and learn little in the brave new economy*. New York: Verso Books.

Pettinger, L. (2004). Brand culture and branded workers: service work and aesthetic labour in fashion retail, *Consumption, Markets and Culture*, 7(2): 165–84.

Piketty, T. (2014). *Capital in the twenty-first century*. Trans. A. Goldhammer, Cambridge: The Belknap Press of Harvard University Press.

Polesel, J., Helme, S., Mason, K & Nicholas, T. (2003). Young Visions Final Report. EORU: University of Melbourne

Pope-Susssman, R. (2012). Unpaid internships should be illegal., *New York Times,* 7 February, https://www.nytimes.com/roomfordebate/2012/02/04/do-unpaid-internships-exploit-college-students/unpaid-internships-should-be-illegal

Pratt, A. G., Ramsden, P. & Peake, L. (2000). *Financing new media: a report for banking on culture.* Liverpool: North West Arts Board.

Pratt, A. & Gill, R. (2008). In the social factory? Immaterial labour, precariousness and cultural work, *Theory, Culture & Society,* 25(7–8): 1–30.

Raban, J. (2008). *Soft city.* London: Pan Macmillan.

Radway, J. A. (1983). Women read the romance: the interaction of text and context, *Feminist Studies,* 9(1): 53–78.

Reckwitz, A. (2017). *The Invention of Creativity,* Cambridge, Polity.

Reich, R. (1991). *The work of nations: preparing ourselves for twenty-first century capitalism.* New York: Alfred Knopf.

Robinson, L. & Lamb, S. (2012). *How young people are faring, 2012.* Melbourne: The Foundation for Young Australians.

Rose, N. (1999). *Governing the Soul.* London: Free Association Books

Ross, A. (2009). *Nice work if you can get it: life and labour in precarious times.* New York: New York University Press.

Sassen, S. (2001). *The global city*: New York, London, Tokyo. Princeton: Princeton University Press.

Scharff, C. (2016). The psychic life of neoliberalism: Mapping the contours of entrepreneurial subjectivity. *Theory, Culture & Society,* 33(6): 107-122.

Sennett, R. (1999). *The corrosion of character: the personal consequences of work in the new capitalism.* New York, London: W.W. Norton & Company

Sennett, R. (2001). 'Street and Office. Two Sources of Identity' in W.Hutton and A.Giddens *On the Edge Living with Global Capitalism,* London: Vintage.

Sennett, R. & Cobb, J. (1972). *The hidden injuries of class.* Cambridge, London, Melbourne: Cambridge University Press.

Shorthose, J. (2004). A more critical view of the creative industries: production, consumption and resistance, *Capital & Class,* 84: 1–10.

Simpson, C. R. (1981). *SoHo, the artist in the city.* Chicago: University of Chicago Press.

Snow, E. (1972). *Red Star Over China.* Harmondsworth: Penguin.

Speers, L. (2015). From artist to entrepreneur: the working lives of London-based rappers, in M. S. Hracs & T. Virani (eds), *The production and consumption of music in the digital age.* London: Routledge.

Standing, G. (2011). *The Precariat: the dangerous new class.* London: Bloomsbury

Stretton, H. (1989). *Ideas for Australian cities.* Sydney: Transit.

TAFE NSW (2014). Smart and Skilled: NSW skills list., http://www.training.nsw.gov.au/form_documents/smartandskilled/skills_list/2014_skills_list_alphabetical_v2.pdf accessed 8 March 2014

Taylor, S. & Littleton, K. (2012). *Contemporary identities of creative labour and creative work.* Aldershot: Ashgate

Thompson, E. P. (1963). *The making of the english working class.* London: Victor Gollancz Ltd.

Thornton, S. (1995). *Club cultures: music, media, and subcultural capital.* Cambridge: Polity.

Throsby, D. & Zednik, A. (2010). *Do you really expect to get paid: an economic study of professional artists in Australia.* Sydney: Australian Council for the Arts.

Turner, F. (2006). *From counterculture to cyberculture: Stewart Brand, the Whole Earth Network, and the rise of digital utopianism.* Chicago: University of Chicago Press.

Virno, P. (1996). Virtuosity and revolution: the political theory of exodus, in P. Virno & M. Hardt (eds), *Radical thought in Italy: a potential politics.* Minneapolis: University of Minnesota Press.

Vosko, L. F., MacDonald, M. & Campbell, I. (2009). *Gender and the contours of precarious employment.* London: Routledge.

Walkerdine, V. (2003). Reclassifying upward mobility: femininity and the neo-liberal subject, *Gender and Education*, 15(3): 237–48.

Warhurst, C. (2010). The missing middle: management in the creative industries, in B. Townley & M. Beech (eds), *Managing creativity: exploring the paradox.* Cambridge: Cambridge University Press.

Warhurst, C. & Nickson, D. P. (2007). A new labour aristocracy? Aesthetic labour and routine interactive service, *Work, employment and society*, 21(4): 785–98.

Warhurst, C. & Nickson, D. P. (2001). *Looking good, sounding right: style counselling in the new economy.* London: The Industrial Society.

Watson, I. (2015). *A disappearing world: studies in class, gender and memory.* Melbourne: Australian Scholarly Publishing

Watson, I., Buchanan, J., Campbell, I. & Briggs, C. (2003). *Fragmented futures: new challenges in working life.* Sydney: Federation Press.

Weissman, J. (2012). Our low-wage recovery: how mcJobs have replaced middle class jobs., *The Atlantic*, 31 August, http://www.theatlantic.com/business/archive/2012/08/our-low-wage-recovery-how-mcjobs-have-replaced-middle-class-jobs/261839/

Wenger, E. (1998). *Communities of practice.* Cambridge: Cambridge University Press

Williams, R. (1988). Keywords. London: Fontana.

Willis, P. (1977). *Learning to labour: how working class kids get working class jobs.* Farnborough, Eng: Saxon House

Wright, E. O. (2006). Two redistributive proposals – universal basic income and stakeholder grants, *In Focus*, 24(2): 5–7.

Wyn, J. (2004). Becoming adult in the 2000s, *Family Matters*, 68: 6–12.

ZDNet (2011). British PM: London's Tech City now has over 600 firms., Retrieved from http://www.zdnet.com/article/british-pm-londons-tech-city-now-has-over-600-firms/

Zukin, S. (1989). *Loft living: culture and capital in urban change.* New Jersey: Rutgers University Press.

Zwick, D. & Cayla, J. (eds) (2011). *Inside marketing: practices, ideologies and devices.* Oxford: Oxford University Press.

INDEX